Teaching Children's Gymnastics

ⁿRSITY⁰F

Dedications

I would like to dedicate this book to my college teacher Mrs. Irma Nikolai, born Lenzing. Mrs. Irma Nikolai was a member of the Mettmanner Gymnastics Club since the age of seven. She was German Gymnastics Champion in the all-around competition and was a member of the 1936 Olympic Team. Since 1938, she was coached by Hermann Ohnesorg at the Reichs Academy for Physical Education in Berlin. He is considered the father of children's gymnastics. With the foundation of the German College of Sports in 1947 she was called to Cologne by Carl Diem as one of the first to serve as college professor. Until 1978, the year of her retirement, she trained thousands of sports students. Natural gymnastics, children performing gymnastics on apparatus and helping each other, cooperating with each other and humanity; her basic thoughts and lessons are contained in this book.

Dedicated to Kea, Jasper, Steffen and Henryk, representing all children of this world.

Above all dedicated to my parents Emmi and Werner Busse, who unselfishly did everything for us children in order to give us the best foundation and prerequisites for our lives. They helped wherever they could. They participated in our lives and always gave us the security of a parental home, which we wish for all children.

Thanks

I would like to thank my colleague Jürgen Engler very much for his unending support in the foundation phase of this book, and Mariette Mahkorn who was a big help during the final stage. Last but not least, I would like to thank my friend of many years, Achim Fassbender, very much for the translation of this book. He accepted, as a graduate from the German College of Sports, based on his experiences as gymnastics coach in Germany and the United States, the difficult task of translating subject specific literature from German into English. Thank you, finally, to Michelle Meyer, who read and corrected the book again in 2009.

Cologne, Ilona E. Gerling

Ilona E. Gerling

Teaching Children's Gymnastics

Spotting and Securing

Step by step with thousands of ideas
for children to spot each other

Meyer & Meyer Sport

Please observe: The author and the publisher do not assume any
responsibility for injuries that might occur when putting exercises or
spotting grips, which are listed in this book, into practice.

Original title: Kinder Turnen – Helfen und Sichern
– Aachen: Meyer und Meyer Verlag, 1997
Translation by Achim Fassbender

British Library Cataloguing in Publication Data
A catalogue record for this book is available from the British Library

Teaching Children's Gymnastics
Ilona E. Gerling
Maidenhead: Meyer & Meyer Sport (UK) Ltd., 1998
2nd, revised edition 2009
ISBN: 978-1-84126-276-5

© 1998 by Meyer & Meyer Sport (UK) Ltd.
2nd, revised edition 2009
Aachen, Adelaide, Auckland, Budapest, Cape Town, Graz, Indianapolis,
Maidenhead, Olten (CH), Singapore, Toronto
Member of the World
Sport Publishers' Association (WSPA)
www.w-s-p-a.org
Printed by: B.O.S.S Druck und Medien GmbH
ISBN: 978-1-84126-276-5
E-Mail: info@m-m-sports.com
www.m-m-sports.com

Contents

How to Use This Book

This book not only contains the descriptions and illustrations of spotting grips, but it also tries to make this vast and important subject matter more clear for those who are involved with spotting in gymnastics. It's my wish with this book to give practical aid for better comprehension and transfer into practice to those who would like to gain further knowledge in gymnastics, as well as those who carry out the instruction.

I hope you will not allow yourself to be scared away by so much theory in order to put the theory of children spotting each other into action. Even though the idea of spotting each other might be quite unusual for the children at first effort is worthwhile. Once this form of teaching is tried and put into practice, every participant will recognize that it's very easy and lots of fun.

Aspects of the subject matter at the beginning of this book will inform the teacher WHAT "spotting" is, and HOW it is done well. The pedagogical, psychological and sociological aspects try to explain WHY "spotting" of the children amongst themselves is so valuable. In theory you will find hundreds of suggestions for lessons/practices that improve the idea of children spotting each other, as well as practical examples that show the children step by step how to spot each other, all well explained with pictures.

The last part of the book is the representation and illustration of spotting grips for immediate consultation for instructional preparation. For coaches, as well as for teachers at school, this book is equally valuable for the directors of day camps or circus projects because it also informs through examples – including trick skills from acrobatics, tumbling, balancing or trapeze – all these fields.

It's up to you where and how you start to read this book; it's certainly a valuable partner for your gymnastics lessons.

Lots of fun in gymnastics!
Yours, Ilona Gerling

Preface:
Spotting and Securing is More!

"Spotting and Securing" is without a doubt a decisive prerequisite for danger free and successful gymnastics on equipment. Therefore, it is a "means to an end" for facilitating movement learning and reducing possible fears.

But couldn't "Spotting and Securing" be more?! I think so! Let's take a look at what is going on here. Someone entrusts his body and life confidently into someone else's while trying a new artistic trick. And this person responds to this act of trust with unrestricted responsibility, to first prevent severe damage to that person, and beyond that to facilitate a moment of success.

What's happening here on a psycho-social level is more than a technical procedure. This requires an attitude of mutual give and take, a challenge to act responsibly, which promotes interaction and cooperation, it strengthens the perception of togetherness and the experience of unity.

This all relates to social virtues that, in a materialistic world, where people are on an EGO trip and insatiably need to satisfy their hunger under the motto 'immediate gratification', need to be revitalized. The social impulses that are generated through 'Spotting and Securing' can contribute here.

This is why I, as sports educator and President of the German Gymnastics Federation (Deutscher Turner Bund = DTB) welcome this book. It links well with the efforts of the DTB to, on the one hand make the meaning and possibilities of social aspects increasingly visible, and on the other to give practical help for social interaction.

The author Ilona Gerling, who is the Federal Chairperson for Gymnastics in the DTB and an instructor at the German College of Sports in Cologne (Deutsche Sporthochschule = DSHS Köln), has, based on her tremendous foundation of knowledge and vast experience, written this book that exemplifies that 'Spotting and Securing' is more. I wish this book success, especially since it addresses the subject of children and because our world of tomorrow needs more social responsibility.

Prof. Dr. Jürgen Dieckert
President of the German
Gymnastics Federation (DTB)

Introduction: From the Jahn-ish "Help" to Children Spotting

> Through helping
> one wins friends.
> To allow being helped
> is a proof of friendship.

Spotting and securing – who in gymnastics doesn't know these two terms that are mentioned in one breath and simply belong to this sport? Most people though still associate these terms exclusively as requirements to be used with the learning and successful execution of a new skill, such as a pullover, or front and back handspring.

Looking back into history, spotting and securing was primarily seen as a purpose for movement support and securing. After the "Deutsche Turnkunst" (German Artistic Gymnastics) was published by Ludwig Jahn and Ernst Eiselen in 1816, "the usefulness of good illustrations should not be taken for granted" and it "was mutually accepted, that this row of illustrations be updated significantly and put in order, and be set into a more decisive accord and relationship with the new edition of the 'Deutsche Turnkunst'" (Eiselen 1889).

The idea of the first published "Illustrations of Gymnastics Exercises" in 1848, edited by E. Eiselen, was thus born. It not only contained 400 illustrations of gymnastics poses and exercises, but there were also many impressive illustrations about "spotting", spotting grips, and safety positions. Many of today's spotting grips resemble those from the past. We find the securing of the wrists for hip circles, the fixation of the knee bend and lifting of the body's center of gravity when swinging in a knee hang, the support grip, turn grips, push-turn assistance and even illustrations for safety positions (see Fig. I-IX, p. 17 and picture legend, p. 239). The book is still, to this day, a treasure chest for every coach. Skills like neck kip, seat circle und knee hang swing that have been ousted from modern gymnastics, belong then and today to the artistic gymnastics tricks of the children and thus in the gymnastics class.

These tricks that can be demonstrated develop naturally out of the children's unrestricted movement. Here the children not only give themselves tips and ideas during common play, but also mutual assistance. For example, when children are ready to learn a handstand out of their own motivation, they are also ready to assist each other. Even though Eiselen's illustrations showed older spotters, assisting each other has always been applied during natural (gymnastics) play amongst children. As part of the children's skill repertoire, tuned in with their learning experience in the area of movement, assistance, occurs very naturally in the world of children.

As it used to be in Jahn's times, good spotting compensated for conditional shortcomings. It enables training a certain unachieved skill with endless practice repetitions. Spotters can thus slow down the movement, support and guide it, so that the gymnast gains an idea about the movement pattern.

Mutual spotting also comprises many demands that stimulate development in many areas. Starting with the coordinated teaching of watching a movement and judging it, they further the cognitive exploration with movements, extended attention span, the ability to concentrate and to react, and last but not least increased strength of the entire body.

The organizational aspect in school and gymnastics clubs for a successful gymnastics lesson is also dependent upon the inclusion of mutual spotting and securing. Can children spot children? Can they work in small groups? Many – also diversified – stations can be set up where the children can practice without waiting. Each child can be immediately taken care of by all the other children individually, with more or less help, with correction and praise. The new pedagogical ideas for gymnastics that propagate the process-oriented open teaching forms are also dependent upon such concepts. Unrestricted gymnastics, group or synchronized gymnastics, experiencing movement possibilities in day camps, circus demonstrations on the trapeze, on the rope, on the balancing ball or building pyramids in the acrobatic group; with the children's ability to spot each other, such ideas can be successfully realized. This exemplifies how, within the play community in the playground, with each child dependent upon the spotting of someone else, mutual spotting of each other contains more values than "just being lifted".

In modern children's gymnastics at school and in the clubs such processes that include mutual spotting are supported. They are of inestimable value for personal development as well as for learning cooperation. What's being developed through mutual spotting by the children is more than merely technical assistance for the realization of a movement.

To help not only means helping others, but also receiving help. Reciprocal spotting in small groups means working with each other instead of against each other. In such work groups the children become a "team" in which they can make achievements together. This requires and strengthens communication, cooperation, problem solving, conflict regulating, the ability to listen and observe and also the acceptance of different opinions through action. Children and youths want to co-decide and co-create, they also want to learn naturally to accept responsibilities. Independence and the ability to act on their own grow with such experience. We need to provide them with the appropriate conditions to prove themselves in such environments.

To spot someone means to accept responsibility for someone, to accept assistance is a matter of trust. "To dare" depends then on "to trust someone". Inhibitory processes are diminished in such common interactions. Mutual spotting presumes being comfortable with placing "hands-on" another child, and allowing "hands on" from another child; there is constant body contact. They are constantly encouraged and praised, they laugh, fears are overcome. Increasingly a "We-feeling" evolves.

Under such conditions many achieve moments of success, and successes motivate, strengthen self-awareness and help to develop a strong personality. Children need such opportunities while growing up. Video games instead of ball games, internet surfing instead of horse play, TV rooms instead of play rooms mark the world of today's children. They are being made aware by a "cell phone and internet world" instead of their own world of discovery. Cyber space and techno music irritate and change the ability for perception without them being conscious of it, and they can destroy the ability to form relationships with others. Today's world of excess doesn't present value feelings anymore. The "single life" of the children in a world where everything is "do-able" propagates loneliness. Human warmth and closeness and having fun together are being sought, and are inestimably valuable. The parents, by way of example, the educators in pre-school and kindergarten, coaches in the clubs and those teaching in the schools, all can contribute in that regard for those growing up.

Two hundred years ago spotting by Jahn's and Eiselen's gymnasts served in the first place as a way of "assisting" to achieve or secure a skill, in today's world there are new values to be derived out of this. To experience life and to live with one another is, in the world of today's children, more urgent then ever. Mutual spotting and accepting being spotted in gymnastics is a contribution to these values.

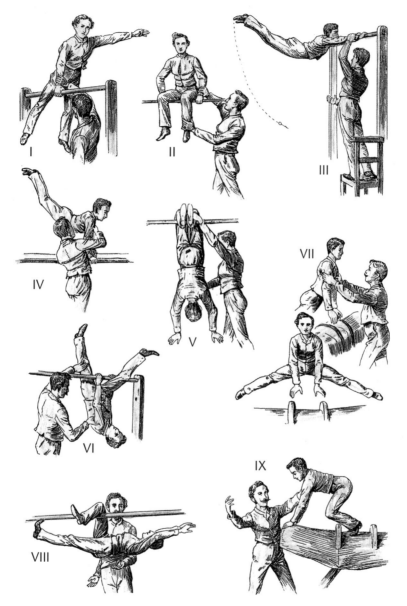

From:
Eiselen, E. W. B. (publisher): Abbildungen von Turn-Übungen, 5. Auflage von Wasser-mannsdorff, K., Verlag Georg Reimer, Berlin 1889, Ill. - Nr. 70, 101, 142, 203, 231, 232, 236, 248, (Terms for the exercises see appendix page 239)

A   THEORY: SPOTTING MEANS ...

> Spotting means: "To have everything under control
> and always be ready for the student!"
> Movement accompaniment means:
> "To be part of it means everything!"
> Securing is: "...to be the guardian angel!"

I.   Aspects of the Subject Matter

Spotting and securing accompanies the child in gymnastics at all levels of the learning process, from learning a new skill, to continued practicing, to practical forms of application (see also Fig. B, p. 22). When children assist each other, children's gymnastics will be enriched for the little ones through an infinite number of new experiences. That is why partner-oriented assistance is to be understood equally as an experience and a learning field, next to learning the gymnastics movements and should be a permanent part of children's gymnastics.

The teacher's, and consequently the child's, knowledge about spotting often leaves much to be desired. There are no theories that describe the inclusion of spotting for practice (except maybe the knowledge that a child can't get up, attempt a pullover or something similar, and thus spotting becomes necessary), or a book that delivers explanations and illustrations about spotting, that make this huge system of actions more clear. Why and how will be shown in the following.

1   Definition of Terms: Spotting – Movement Accompaniment – Securing

In the general, linguistic-specific application, spotting and securing is named in one breath. In practice the teacher may place a "safety spotter" behind the vault, but expects "active spotting" from one person. Spotters will

"assist" during a high bar routine, but in gymnastics a little push here or there may suffice and requires "finger tip sensitivity".

Thus, there is no need for forceful support, nor does the spotter have to stand around waiting. In order to competently learn and teach the complexity of the more or less, or the no longer needed spot, requires at first an explanation of the different actions through terminology definitions.

Spotting can be differentiated into three forms and can therefore be defined as follows:

Spotting
is generally understood as **actively** supporting the movement. Thus, movement support is goal-oriented, active, stepping in behavior.

We talk about **Movement Accompaniment/Guiding**
when the hands accompany the course of the movement of the body without intending a steady and active support:
as much as necessary – as little as possible!

Securing
is described as merely **observing** behavior, as the readiness to step in effectively when problems arise during the realization of the movement. In the event of emergency, it serves as **accident prevention**.

Fig. A: Spotting – Movement Accompaniment/Guiding – Securing

The application of spotting as movement support and guidance, movement accompaniment and movement securing, is dependent upon the situation and the degree of skill ability of the gymnasts, as can be concluded from Fig. B, p. 22.

2   Explanations and Practice Examples

From the definition it becomes clear that spotting has a prerequisite character for movement accompaniment and again for the ability to secure, which means that only experienced spotters can secure safely. This additionally means that qualified, reliable securing is needed at the highest ability level. This securing can be learned through the next lower ability level of movement accompaniment.

Here standards evolve as well as learning levels for spotting. Assisting in the original sense (accompanying and securing) is, with regard to the practical application, dependent upon the control of the gymnastics skill to be performed.

Also learning to assist and to secure (see chapter A III. 2) is always performed in connection with, and parallel to the learning of gymnastics-specific basics and skills. This coherence is exemplified in the next overview (Fig. B, p. 22).

- **Spotting:** For new skills to be learned, assisting is a form of manual movement support in order to compensate for weaknesses in condition and coordination, as well as guiding the movement in order to correct the course of the movement and improving the visualization of the movement. Through this partner supported guidance the gymnast – and the assisting child – get to know the new movement to be learned.

Fig. 1: Spotting a pullover

Examples:

- Pullover on a bar: While the gymnast is standing still, the spotters already reach with both hands for the seat and direct the center of gravity on the shortest way to the bar. By carrying the body weight, the practicing gymnast is relieved and can repeatedly practice the pullover, despite a lack of holding strength in the hands, pull strength of the arms or abdominal strength (Fig. 1).

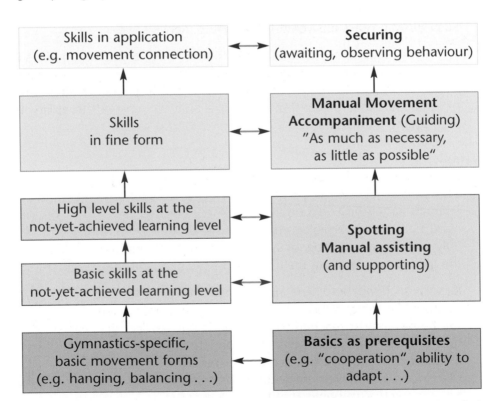

Skills in application (e.g. movement connection)	**Securing** (awaiting, observing behaviour)
Skills in fine form	**Manual Movement Accompaniment** (Guiding) "As much as necessary, as little as possible"
High level skills at the not-yet-achieved learning level	**Spotting Manual assisting** (and supporting)
Basic skills at the not-yet-achieved learning level	
Gymnastics-specific, basic movement forms (e.g. hanging, balancing . . .)	**Basics as prerequisites** (e.g. "cooperation", ability to adapt . . .)

Fig. B: Simplified illustration of the standard and learning levels in the area of skills with the inclusion of spotting, manual movement accompaniment and securing

- Cast to handstand: Due to a lack of support strength the spotters guide the gymnast at the thighs into the vertical and lift him with a support grip on the thighs. Thus, the strength required from the gymnast for a front support is reduced, meaning the child carries significantly less of his body weight, depending on the amount of spotting.

- **Accompanying:** The transition from spotting to accompanying a movement is smooth. Movement guidance decreases steadily, the movement gets gentle support only in partial phases following the principle "as much as necessary, as little as possible" (Fig. 2). This demands from all participants an evaluation of the entire situation and everything that's part of the action (refer also to chapters B 3 on Prerequisites, p. 25-51). How far is the gymnast ability-wise? How consistent is the gymnast's efficiency? Where are the problems during the course of practice? How do I have to act in surprise situations . . .? Such questions are answered through experience.

To reliably accompany a course of movement and especially routines is the result of long spotting experience. To accompany movements smoothly means to possess experience in spotting. The children thus need to be prepared long-term for the goal to achieve the ability to accompany a movement.

Examples:
- Pullover on bars: The spotters do not reach for the seat while the gymnast is still in preparation, but only when the gymnast has already reached an inverted position. Instead of using both hands, a slight pushing assistance is now given only with one hand, depending on the improved standard of the gymnast, by pushing the hips against the bar.

- Kick up to handstand: The spotters do not reach for the thighs while the gymnast is in preparation, but only when she/he has almost reached the vertical. In the vertical the spotter's grip is loosened again and again to see if the gymnast can establish balance on her/his own. With increasing movement security the spotters accompany the up-swing and the holding of the handstand with their "fingertips"(Fig. 2).

Fig. 2

In the end the accompaniment of the movement leads to gymnastics without spotting during the course of a movement, and therefore it turns into securing.

■ **Securing:** In order to secure the gymnast it's assumed that the gymnast can execute the skill without movement accompaniment. The spotters' hands do not accompany the body of the practicing gymnast. The course of the movement is observed attentively in an accompanying manner by the securing person.

If the securing persons assume that at one point during the course, or in a partial phase of the movement, the skill won't work, they step in to save the gymnast. Therefore the securing person must know the characteristics of the movement, the problematic phases of the skill, and must also be able to use the necessary spotting grip.

Examples:

• For dismounts off the apparatus and for supported vaults we secure the landings by catching the gymnast at his back and front and "forking" him in (Fig. 3). Increasingly the securing of the landing is only hinted at and a spotter merely remains ready to catch the gymnast in case of a fall.

Additionally, securing is fundamentally applied

– when practicing the fine form of a movement,
– when applying the skills in connections,
– during movement creation,
– when incorporating the learned skills into game and competition formats.

Based on the above explanations the field of application has been divided into three standard levels. Spotting, movement accompaniment and securing can be learned step by step in each of these standard levels. Section A III. 2 (p. 62-69) describes this extensively.

Fig. 3: Securing a landing

3   Prerequisites

3.1   Conditioning and Coordination Abilities

Good spotting and securing requires different prerequisites from the children. Through preparatory exercises (see section B I. 1, p. 71-129) on the one hand basics for spotter actions are created, and on the other hand different abilities are trained and knowledge is gained through assisting and securing.

Conditioning and coordination abilities determine the degree of quality of the assistance. The following examples have been chosen for demonstrating conditioning and coordination abilities.

Condition: Strength and Quickness

- **Strength (power, force)**

To move the body weight of a gymnast against gravity, in order to carry the body onto a bar, to lift over the hands into a handstand, or to redirect, or erect the body, as in a squat, straddle and pike vault just prior to landing, demands a great amount of strength from those spotting. A small, slender child should not have to lift or carry the largest, strongest child in the group.

For this reason, when groups are formed, in order to spot each other, the arrangement of the children according to the body height and weight must be checked and if necessary corrected by the teacher.

Supporting, lifting, carrying and at times even the catching of the body weight (often made more difficult through acceleration), requires one not to underestimate the need for maximum strength potential. Because movements in swing-oriented gymnastics need to be dynamically supported, quickness is asked for in order to be able to optimally assist. For those strength inputs it is not only the arm, but also the shoulder, torso and leg musculature that is of importance. In order to lift a partner during a pullover at a bar at head height, the lifting of the arms is necessary. The torso musculature is stabilized so that the spotter doesn't tilt forward during the lift. The lift gets completed through the extension of the legs and hips. Through the act of spotting, the musculature of the entire body gets trained. Isometric and surmountable (concentric) holding power, as well as negative, resistant (eccentric) muscle work is produced.

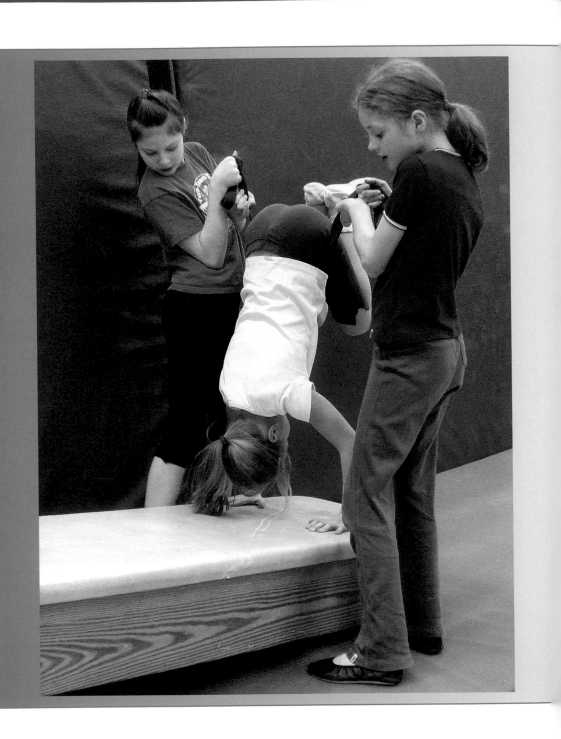

Do not forget, there is a demand for a vertebrae stabilizing holding force of the torso during supportive strength inputs. Forceful spotting on the other hand leads as stimulation to the development of this vertebrae stabilizing torso strength, through the manifold strains on the entire torso musculature. Thus, the assisting activity of the children can be regarded as posture education. One may assume that additional stimulation of the bones occurs, positively influencing bone density and bone statics in the developmental stages of the child.

■ **Speed**

Especially in movement connections spotter grips must be applied or changed in fast succession, often, as for example for an under-swing on bars the spotter grips change even within the movement. The gymnast gets carried into distance underneath the shoulder and seat. The hand, spotting the seat, changes shortly before landing to the front of the shoulder in order to prevent a fall forward (Fig. 4).

Fig. 4: Under-swing: Speed in changing the spotters' grip

Additionally the following along during spotting, as is necessary during support vaults, requires sufficient movement speed from the spotters.

An example:
During a squat vault it often happens that a gymnast gets caught with his feet at the edge of the box. Within a fraction of a second the gymnast needs to be grabbed and caught. This requires quick reactions from the accompanying spotter or securer. For that reason the children can start the beginning of practice with reaction games as a preparation for the following spotting techniques.

Action speed (movement speed) is especially demanded for guiding movement assistance. A seat circle for example must be spotted with the far hand that reaches very quickly underneath the shoulder girdle in order to lift the gymnast to a sitting position. If numerous seat circles are performed in a row, the securing of the close grip must be released very quickly so that one can reach back underneath the bar and back to the wrist. The gymnast's wrist needs to be tightly and quickly secured each time (Fig. 194/195, p. 209).

Coordination: Regulated Strength Input, Skillfulness, Adaptability, Connecting, Combination and Rhythmic Ability

From a physiological perspective, movement coordination is defined as the interaction of the central nervous system and the skeletal musculature, within a specific course of a movement.

Aiming at a purpose or a set goal, one strives for movement precision and economy through time, space and strength optimized body control. It is expected during spotting for one to be highly coordinated and precise while working under time pressure.

Aside from the abilities for equilibrium, orientation and reaction, and to further the motor learning ability, the following terms are also explanatory for steering actions during spotting. Important coordination abilities, like the ability to differentiate, should be added. Almost all coordination abilities are partially, in no insignificant dimension, contained in the following.

■ Regulated strength input

The children must be able to handle the assisting strength input, according to the situation, in various strength degrees. A pullover for example must not be spotted with too much strength, because in this case the gymnast might be thrown with his hips onto the bar (Fig. 5).

For the knee hang swings, the pressing down of the lower legs assures the knee flexion for the knee hang. If this happens too forcefully, it can cause pain for the gymnast (Fig. 6).

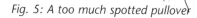

Fig. 5: A too much spotted pullover

Fig. 6: Painful knee hang swing with too much pressing down

■ Skillfulness and differentiation abilities

Skillfulness here describes coordination abilities in time-space and dynamic differentiation abilities.

Examples:

• Reaching for the upper arms during a squat or straddle vault demands an agility in the form of well-timed, target-oriented grabbing, and an effective, strength appropriate action – in this case – through the use of a support grip (see Fig. 150, p. 181 and Fig. 151, 154-156, p. 181-183).

- Same works for the knee hang swing. The grip that secures the knee hang needs to be released in the final phase, in order to, then, quickly turn the hand to the back and prevent the gymnast from falling backwards (Fig. 200 and 201, p. 211 f.).

- Or: when rolling out of a handstand, the hands that held the thighs are released in order to reach underneath the arms and help the gymnast to stand up (Fig. 7).

Fig. 7: Rolling out of a handstand: Quickly changing the spotter grip

A rudimentary motor skillfulness is required as a foundation for good spotting, which requires very *sensitive neuromuscular adaptation*. The quality of the ability to differentiate depends on, amongst other things, how far the kinesthetic perception is developed. The ability for *kinesthetic perception*, which means "feel", how far a joint is bent or stretched, and how tense the muscles are, can be taught through frequent feedback (too much/not enough), through the action result or from outside, through verbal feedback from other children or the teacher. These practice situations are again created through spotting actions.

■ Adaptability

Adaptability is an *ability to anticipate* and, in case of surprise, an *ability to convert or re-adjust*. This means that in a complex gymnastic situation spotters in general should be able to anticipate distances, movement speed, dynamics and the amplitude of movements, mistakes within the movement

and emotional reaction to errors, as well as estimating and reacting to equipment reactions (mini-tramp). Good, solid knowledge, as described in this chapter, forms the prerequisites for good adaptation ability. Additionally, the spotters should be sensitized to what could happen during the execution of a movement. Focal points for observation that are given by the teacher/coach should teach the best way to watch a movement for the necessary adaptation ability during spotting. With regard to different demand structures, the adaptation ability in spotting procedures can be divided into three areas:

- **Adaptation to the gymnast:** Each child is different, consequently also in movement conduct. The spotters need to adjust to this. A quiet child will perform an exercise differently from a excitable child. Each one has his own movement rhythm. Additionally, we look at emotional conditions that can influence the execution of movements. When kicking up to a handstand the gymnast must be approached, whereas in case of slowly or hectic swung arms a stepping away may be necessary before the gymnast can be helped. Spotting a turn-over backward "salto" from a forward run on the swinging rings requires the spotters to wait and see where the gymnast is going to release before the spotter can direct the movement. The timid child jumps early and is very hesitant, without self-confidence, the gutsy child jumps very late and partially, uncontrollably fast. Verbal remarks already give hints as to what to expect. The call: "Hold me!" expresses an emotional condition. The child is afraid of the skill. Body language also reflects the world of emotions of a gymnast. Rubbing wet hands against the hips expresses nervousness. This is supposed to teach specific movement observation in order to recognize dispositions of the gymnast. *Spotter adaptation abilities* are *especially necessary for movement accompaniment and securing.*

- **Adaptation to the course of the movement:** Each movement is different with regard to its movement qualities in terms of movement distance, height, rhythm and flow. The spotters often act erroneously in their attempt to steer the movement. They may lift too high or won't let the child lower down sufficiently while they hold against or push the legs or the center of gravity too quickly in the wrong direction. It's not always the lack of knowledge that spoils the ideal execution, but it can be the lack of alertness wanting to steer and direct a skill.

An example:
An under-swing should primarily be executed with distance. The spotters should therefore not lift the gymnast too forcefully. Because the gymnast executes the skill according to the given norm (respectively his visualization of the course of the movement), he would in this case (because of sudden fear development) be surprised by the height, trying to get the legs back down quickly to the floor for landing, and therefore, because of the height, pull the legs underneath his body, which could cause him to flip forward. *Adaptability, when striving for an optimal course of movement, is first and foremost important during supported and guided spotting. The spotters need to have good knowledge about the course of the movement.*

- **Adaptation to the co-spotters:** Last but not least, the spotters amongst themselves need to be able to adapt. Different body heights and strength inputs of the spotting children, or different timing during the spot, can be obstructive rather than helpful. If one spotter lifts stronger during an under-swing than the other, or pulls stronger and longer on one arm during a squat vault, or if a taller child lifts, the spotted gymnast during a "Napoleon" higher than the other spotter, the gymnast may start to twist around his longitudinal axis and land tilted. *In the initial skill learning phase, practice is often done with two or more spotters, where the adaptability toward the co-spotter is decisive for the development of movement imagination and the harmonious success of the course of the movement during supportive and directed spotting.*

■ **Connecting ability**

With regard to this ability, partial body movements of the most different types need to be combined and coordinated. When spotting, thebody joints must work "counter-equal", for example the knee, hip and shoulder joint. One arm may be straightened while simultaneously the other is bent, and the hip and shoulder joints straighten together at the same time. *Small children and spotters are at first not capable of executing complex spotting actions. They should grab with both hands at the same spot and keep their hands there without any grip changes until the movement is finished.*

Examples:

Smaller children and beginner spotters can often help more effectively by grabbing the upper arms with a "turn-grip". Even if the "turn-carry-grip" at the shoulder (between neck and upper arm) and the body's center of gravity (seat) would be a more optimal way to spot and steer a handspring movement, we, nevertheless, ensure reliably that at least the upper body and the head are held up with the different way of spotting at a lower level.

1   2   3   4   5

Figure 8.1-8.5: Spotting grip for handspring movement

Another example shall illustrate the connecting ability in its complexity during spotting. It's difficult for beginners to execute the spotting grip for handspring movements (such as front handspring or neck kip). The closer arm of the spotter must bend and reach for the upper arm/shoulder. The far arm is straight and carries the seat in support of the body's center of gravity. The closer spotter leg is bent, the other is straight (Fig. 8.1-8.2). Beginners quite often tend to straighten both of their arms and both legs, or bend both arms and legs. With the handspring movement, both legs are straightened, the far, straight arm is bent to lower the center of gravity, the other arm must be straightened in order to push the gymnast's upper body into the vertical. Beginning spotters forget in this movement phase to straighten the closer arm in order to erect the upper body. Or they leave the far arm straight and do not lower the center of gravity; a raising of the upper body then becomes complicated. If both legs are bent, they will unknowingly remain bent during the carrying of the gymnast, and thus sag under the load of the body weight of the practicing gymnast. When landing, the second leg begins to bend again in order to place the rotating person back on his feet (Fig. 8). In case the spotters remain "stiff", the flipping person falls onto his feet. *Connecting ability possesses efficiency determined character, particularly for the spotting activities of supporting and guiding.*

■ **Combination ability**

When single movement actions are combined into a bigger situation, a motor combination ability is demanded. Combination ability is required for executing spotting actions of a higher level. This becomes evident when one hand comes into action a little later than the other. Or even clearer, when a spotting grip has to be applied and changed numerous times in a movement combination (for example during continuous back hip circles). Good spotting abilities are shown by those who can apply different spotting grips for diverse skills in an exercise (Fig. 105.1-105.6, p. 148; Fig.116.1-116.14, p. 157-159). Combination ability has prerequisite characteristics, especially for movement accompaniment. It improves through practical application.

■ **Rhythmic ability**

A spotter must know and adequately transform the rhythm and the dynamics of a skill that he intends to influence during movement support. This becomes especially clear on the vaulting events. For a straddle vault the upper body needs to be held almost static, with a support grip on the upper arms, in order to slow it down, and to reerect the upper body energetically right before the landing. The comprehension of movement rhythm is also seen in movement connections. The spotters have to adapt to the different rhythms of the skills, intermediate swings (high bar and parallel bars) and extra steps (floor and beam), in order not to break the flow of the movement.

The aforementioned examples illustrate that spotter activities often demand prerequisites that can pose problems even to teachers and coaches. Therefore, the passing on of fundamental knowledge and frequent practice is of utmost importance.

3.2 Knowledge: About the Technique of Spotting

A certain "knowledge" is indispensable for effective, supportive, steering and accompanying assistance, also for securing the course of the movement. Teachers and coaches alike should acquire the knowledge to train children to become good spotters.

Spotting and Movement Characteristics of a Skill

Movement characteristics are the "cue points" of a course of movement. They are considered the "key" to successfully achieve an artistic skill. Within the characteristics of a movement there is a hierarchy, as to how important they are for the success. A "core movement" forms the point of initiation for everything that follows.

Example:
For a back hip circle, the center of gravity (in front of the hips) must be kept at the axis of rotation (the bar). For spotting we thus need to use both hands in order to keep the center of gravity at the bar.

It's similar for the pullover. The center of gravity needs to be brought to the bar the shortest possible way. Again, the spotters assist and guide under the seat center of gravity) onto the bar. Should the legs not make it over the bar during this movement, but stay vertical in the air, then the spotters assist by pushing against the thighs. The gymnast knows what to do, because of the tactile correction by the spotters.

Achieving a skill successfully depends generally upon a good start to the movement. If possible, assistance should already start during the inital phase.

Example:
When kicking up to a handstand, the assisting hands reach for the thighs during the initial phase of the up-swing, and support the elevation of the center of gravity over the hands through swing leg support.

For rolling onto a box the assisting hands reach around the thighs when the gymnast is just about to make contact with the board, and carry the center of gravity, during the rolling on, over the head. The correction of mistakes therefore complies with the proper or improper execution of the given, typical movement characteristics.

> From here we may conclude that spotters who want to contribute to success must also possess knowledge about the decisive movement characteristics, just like the ones performing them, in order to be able to support, steer and correct successfully.

This is generally the case in a training process, where roles between gymnast and spotter are frequently changed. It is, therefore, not wise to use an "outside person" for spotting and securing who is not informed enough; a scene that is often observed in clubs. Without knowledge they cannot spot, and can even pose a hindrance or be a hazard. Spotters who are not well informed can become the cause of accidents, which has happened often before.

> Knowledge about movement characteristics for skills to be spotted is necessary, because they deliver fundamental information
>
> • about the onset of the helping grip
>
> • for the actions during spotting
>
> • about correct location
>
> • for possible problem situations

Spotting and Problem Moments During the Course of a Movement

With the knowledge about "problematic moments" for skills, one can give even more goal-oriented and intense support for spotting. *Especially when securing, attention focuses on these problematic partial phases of a movement,* in order to step in and help if necessary.

Example:

For pullovers, back hip circles, seat and mill circles, when kicking up to a handstand, when squatting into a squat support onto a box or beam, these crucial "problem moments" occur just prior to reaching the vertical, or at the energetic end of the rotation around the support area (bar or hands/floor). The gymnast falls back in the case of insufficient swing or technique, without attaining the desired end position.

> It's not always possible or meaningful to support the swing initiating phase from the beginning. In this case energetic support is required, just prior to reaching the end position, or during movement accompaniment, or if failure is to be expected, at the point when securing requires a sudden spot.

The following basic rules apply with regard to spotter actions that must be taken into consideration when deciding upon which grip to use, the conduct of the spotter and his location.

Onset of Spotting Grips

1. Spotting grips need to be applied **close to the trunk** where there are possibly only a few joints between grip onset and body mass, so that the gymnast can't slip out (examples: reaching around the thighs during a handstand, reaching around the upper arms during support jumps). The body is therefore more easily maneuverable in its movement through the spotters. Also, the spotters' grips **should not aim for a joint, nor should the hands of the spotters have a joint in between them**.

Example:

The arm can be severely stiffened during support jumps while reaching for the upper arm and the wrist, and can cause an injury when trying to catch the falling, accelerating body (exception: squat dismount off the bars, where from a motionless position the arm is used as a lever).

2. When the body is predominantly held by the hands **during rotations around a fixed axis** (for example on bars), the **grip tightness** must be guaranteed through **wrist joint securing**. Additionally, a rotational

support is thus given. Consequently, this aspect differs from the above mentioned basic rule, applying the spotting grip close to the trunk, because another function of spotting steps into the foreground. The hand close to the bar reaches underneath and grabs the wrist from the front (thumb clasps the wrist), the far hand helps to erect the trunk from the front at the shoulder or the upper arm (for example seat circle, Fig. 194, 195, p. 209), or from behind at the height of the shoulder blades (for example mill or single leg circle forward, Fig. 197.2-197.3, p. 210).

Exceptions:
Pullover or back hip circles do not need to be secured by the wrist, because the carrying of the center of gravity by the spotters requires only a minimal amount of hand strength for the gymnast.

3. If the **center of gravity** needs to be brought to or kept by the bar/rail, **both hands** must support at **the seat**. Example: Pullover (Fig. 104, p. 146) or back hip circle (Fig. 116.2-116.3, p. 157). The same goes for when the gymnast needs to be decelerated and carried down.

Example:
Forward roll from front support on bars to a hanging position. The "load arm" should be shortened through bending of the arms to the body. This becomes clear when, during the carrying, lifting and holding, one has to go underneath the load or the center of gravity (Fig. 9, see also the explanations under "choice of location", p. 43 and Garufi 1994, p. 88).

Fig. 9: Spotting underneath the center of gravity

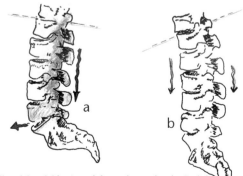

4. If help is necessary **to erect** around the transversal axis in the end phase of a rotary movement (mostly in upward phases), it should happen with a grip onset as **far as possible from the axis of rotation**, in order to take advantage of the lever forces. With the exception of back hip circles, where it is a priority to keep the center of gravity (here the hips) at the axis of rotation (here the bar), circular swings and flips are re-erected at the shoulder girdle, or from the front of the shoulder, with support of the second hand at the center of gravity (as resistive force) (Fig. 10).

Fig. 10: Supporting a gymnast to re-erect him

Body Posture While Lifting and Carrying

Spotter activities demand entire *body involvement*. Someone else's body weight has to be lifted, carried and turned against gravity. Apart from good spotting techniques, one's own body posture needs to be controlled not only for staying healthy, but also for improving the technique.

Fig. 11a-11b: Load from hyperlordosis (a) and on straightened spinal column (b)

A child's normal movement behavior strengthens the entire musculature that stabilizes the vertebrae.

The lifting of the gymnast's body should *start from a slight knee bend*, because leg extension facilitates the lift through the use of the thigh musculature (knee extensor = m. quadriceps femoris).

In contrast to the actual teachings of the "spine specialists", lifting with a *straight back is not advised* for children. Children before puberty show tendencies to "stick out bellies" and thus, show an arched back posture. By following the suggestion of the "spine specialists", to keep the back straight when lifting or carrying, this particular arch back posture may actually increase (hyperlordosis) (Fig. 11a-11b). Apart from that, humans have a natural curvature of the spine in order to support dynamic loads of the body. This is also of importance for spotting.

A much more important hint is to lean slightly forward with the entire trunk when lifting and carrying, and to simultaneously contract the abdominal musculature (m. rectus and m. transversus abdominis)*.

During spotting, the body often has to twist, which includes also a strength involvement of the side abdominals (m. rectus obliquus externus and internus). This corresponds with the child's natural ways of moving. No child, while playing (this also includes for example brother or sister), has lifted or carried something and straightened his back prior to the lift, as if he had swallowed a stick.

"Pulling in the stomach" (without ceasing to breathe), or to lean slightly forward is therefore advised for supportive assistance, rather than to lift and carry "straight like a stick".

Function of the Spotter Grips

The children must not only know the spotting grips and how to correctly apply them at the gymnast's body, but they also need to know how to support and guide the movement meaningfully. Spotter grips can support and carry, lift and push, turn and fixate. The mere onset of the hands on a child doing gymnastics is a spotter grip.

---

* Annotation: One can assume that the internal pressure in the abdominal region, which is generated through the well developed straight, transversal and diagonal "all-around stomach musculature" against the spine, in an all-around covered fasciae, as well as through the well trained spine enclosing muscle groups (for example the back extensor m. erector spinae) in their connective tissue, not only stabilizes the spine (internal muscular pressure), but produces also such a strong external pressure that it acts almost vertical onto the spine when lifting, so that the pressure loads are significantly decreased. Thus, spotting trains the spine supporting musculature in its function.

The children must be shown what they can do with spotter grips, and how they can steer and support.

Examples:

- For a back hip circle, both hands reach for the seat. This onset of the hands is not sufficient information for a successful movement support. With "joined forces of both hands" the body weight is carried to the bar. Prior to that the close hand "transports" the center of gravity from underneath the bar to the bar, the far hand joins slightly later and gently supports the rotation around the bar underneath the seat (Fig. 104, p. 146).

- When kicking up to a handstand, both hands reach around the thigh. It must be clarified that the closer hand assists first the swinging motion of the legs, the far hand prevents the falling over from the vertical (Fig. 129, p. 169).

Spotter Conduct

Principally the following course of action applies to spotting:

1. Spotter grips must be applied **at the earliest possible moment**. Here the helping hands *must go towards the gymnast*. With the beginning of the movement the *view must focus on the part that needs to be reached for or supported* (that means for vaults it starts already with the run) (Fig. 12.1-12.2)!

2. Spotting, movement accompaniment and securing mean **a continuous following along with the movement** of the gymnast. During the course of the movement the spotters need to follow the exact course of

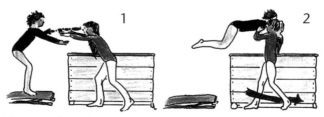

Figure 12.1-12.2

the movement. Exact knowledge about the movement is important. If a movement changes into a (linear) forward motion, or if different skills of an exercise have different problem moments that are in front or behind the bar rail, the spotting must not be permanent at one location, but must change according to the situation (Fig. 105.5-105.6, p. 148).

3. Spotting must take place **until the end of the movement is secured**. Especially for dismounts and vaults over equipment (for example boxes), the attentive holding on to the gymnast, until he reaches a motionless position where he regains his orientation, is important. For under-swings and flips from or over elevations, the fixation of the shoulder girdle is advantageous, because with a long lever arm (distance between grip onset and center of gravity or point of rotation) and good strength input, a falling forward on the landing can be prevented (Fig. 8.1-8.5, p. 33). It's not favorable to catch the landing gymnast at the hips, because the resistance of the helping hands or arms can cause the gymnast to fold in the middle. It's better to grasp the upper arms or to reach for the shoulder blades ("throw out the anchor"). See here the last two photos in the handspring illustration 8.4-8.5, p. 33.

Choice of Location of the Spotter

Knowledge about location and positioning can contribute greatly to the success of spotting.

1. The choice of location in relation to the equipment or gymnast complies with the problem moments derived out of the movement characteristics (see above). In gymnastics the gymnast is constantly interacting with gravity. This shows clearly in the upward directed phases of a movement on high bar and uneven bars. That is where the location at the apparatus should be, in order to help erect with full body strength.

Examples:

*   For backward movements, pullover, seat and back hip circle, the spotter stands in front of the bar (right where the front of the gymnast points to) – also for back hip circles on the recreational uneven-bars from a long hang position that requires a grip change to the lower bar. Only from this location can the spotters stem themselves against the falling body and redirect it against the lower bar (Fig. 13).

1   2   3

Fig. 13

- In contrast to this, for mill, or single leg circles with forward movements, the spotters stand behind the bar. For locomotion or movement connections the spotters must always make the effort to move to a better, often changed location. This includes frequent training and experience. Teachers and coaches must use their advantage from experience to instruct the spotters.

2. The spotters must learn to stay as close as possible to the equipment or the gymnast without obstructing the gymnast. Only in that manner can a child lift, hold and carry a moving body close to his own body. The "load arm" should be shortened through the bending of the arms against the body. This becomes evident when one has to go underneath the load or the center of gravity (Fig. 9, p. 39) during carrying, lifting and holding (see above). All beginners have problems with understanding this principle. Because of the fear of getting hurt by the gymnast, one often observes that the spotters are standing an arm length away from the one to be spotted. A simple call: "Go get them!" can constantly remind them to stay close to the gymnast.

Examples:

- When turning over forward off a box, the spotters need to hold and turn the gymnast with a turn grip at head height, and keep their arms bent and close to their own body, until the gymnast reaches a standing position. (Fig. 14).

- In a practical teaching situation, the correct positioning by the box is always a problem when it comes to spotting a vault sufficiently well. In

our children's classes we continuously observe that the children stand sideways – instead of directly behind the box. They can just barely reach for the upper arm in a support grip, but a carrying of the gymnast into the direction of the movement, or the prevention of a possible fall, can certainly not be helped from this location. Even when they are told or steered into the right position, the children fall back into standing sideways at the box. Repeated correction is necessary.

Fig. 14

3. For movements **that lead into locomotion**, the spotters need to choose the very location where they assume it to be best to **carry the center of gravity** (flips), **to stop** (dynamic round-off) or to **balance** (handstand). It is often required for the spotters to be close to the gymnast in the main and end phases of a movement.

Example:

When kicking up into a handstand, the spotters need to stand exactly where they assume the hands will be placed in order to balance the gymnast. Thus, they may not be at the same height as the gymnast when he starts the kicking up part of the handstand, because in this case the gymnast moves away. A possible falling over due to too much swing cannot be prevented.

4. For supportive, carrying or pushing support, it's often better when the children stand **underneath the center of gravity**, that means underneath the gymnast. For this reason it makes sense to start from an elevated position or give support from a kneeling position.

Examples:

- Neck kip from a box.

- For pullovers or back hip circles on the bars the skill can only be successful if the spotters are positioned on the side of the bar where the movement is in its upward phase. First of all, that is where the "problem point" for the failure of the movement is, and furthermore, that is where the spotter can position himself *underneath the center of gravity* of the gymnast in order to push him up.

Time Aspects of Spotter Actions

It is not necessary to be with the hands on the gymnast during every single partial phase of the course of the movement (see Garufi 1994, p. 89-90).

Initial intervention: From the beginning, spotter grips are to be set on in a movement supportive manner, when, for example, an up-swinging movement needs to be accelerated. Often the effect of a take-off apparatus (spring board) gets further supported.

Examples:

- When kicking up to a handstand, the spotter's close hand to the gymnast reaches underneath the thigh of the swing leg in order to support the upward motion into the handstand (Fig. 129, p. 169).

- When rolling onto a box the spotters reach for the thighs when the gymnast arrives at the board, in order to carry and push the seat over the head, underneath the center of gravity at take-off.

Main part intervention: In its initial stage the movement is executed without assistance, and the supporting grip is used during the main part of the movement in order to contribute to the success of the execution. Waiting with the spot is advised. This is often necessary in order not to disturb the movement initiation through early intervention.

Examples:

- After lowering into a fleet squat stand or long sit, the gymnast rolls back. Now the spotters reach for the thighs and lift the gymnast to a handstand (Fig. 15).

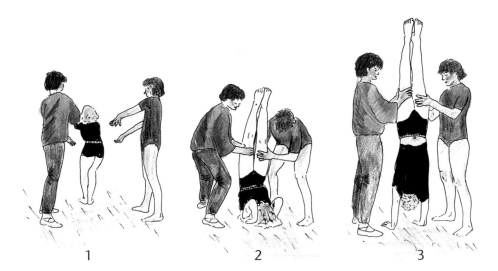

Fig. 15: Main intervention for a backward roll to handstand

- *Seat circle:* The gymnast hangs in the knees, moving backward upward, and lowers himself. The spotter's far hand reaches underneath the hanging point for the shoulder/upper arm in order to support the up-swing phase with a forceful impulse.

Final intervention: In order to force the end of a movement into a motionless position, the spotters reach in, stopping the motion. This is especially the case for dismounts and vaults.

Total intervention: When only a few prerequisites or complex actions within a movement are given, the gymnast is guided and supported through the entire movement (see Garufi 1994, p. 90).

Example:
- Handstand forward roll to straight jump (Fig. 130, 131, p. 170).

Transferability of Spotting Grips and Actions

Many basic learned spotter grips and actions are transferable to other apparatus, especially when dealing with similar skills:

Fig. 16a-c: The same spotter grip and choice of location

- Support grip on the upper arm with shoulder lock when squatting onto a box, a bar or beam . . . (Fig. 16a-c).

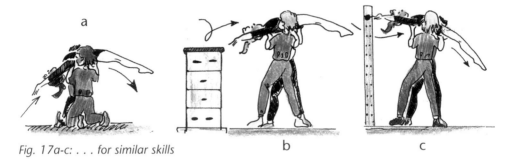

Fig. 17a-c: . . . for similar skills

- Front handspring step out on floor, neck kip from a box, Yamashita over the box . . . (Fig. 17a-c).

Once learned, certain courses of movement for supporting actions are transferable in their sequence to other courses of movement. This relationship should be clarified to the children by the teacher/coach. Assisting action maneuvers thus gain an overview, and become clearer.

As was already stated in the section "spotter conduct" (p. 42), children need to show a certain spotter conduct when spotting.

- With positioning in a certain location for spotting, eye contact is established with the gymnast, and if necessary a verbal agreement is

made. The spotters get ready for applying the grip ("in the air") and the arms extend toward the gymnast.

- During movement initiation the spotter has to move to meet the gymnast.

- There then follows, at the most favorable moment (often the earliest possible), the application of the grip and the movement is supported and guided according to need.

- The grip is applied long enough for the child to reach the final, motionless position. For landings the movement is usually stopped.

The following chart (Fig. C) clarifies these points by illustrating three skills, the transferability of spotter conduct for essential areas, that, judged by their course, can be considered typical for movements in children's gymnastics.

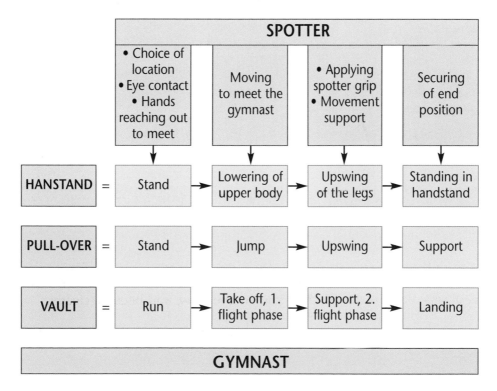

SPOTTER				
• Choice of location • Eye contact • Hands reaching out to meet	Moving to meet the gymnast	• Applying spotter grip • Movement support	Securing of end position	
HANSTAND =	Stand	Lowering of upper body	Upswing of the legs	Standing in handstand
PULL-OVER =	Stand	Jump	Upswing	Support
VAULT =	Run	Take off, 1. flight phase	Support, 2. flight phase	Landing
GYMNAST				

Fig. C: The course of spotter actions during gymnastics movements

"Game Rules" Between Spotters and Gymnasts

Especially for gymnastics with spotting, there are rules for cooperation.

The first rule that should be familiar to all gymnasts refers to **the dress code**. The gymnasts and the spotting children must:

- Remove *watches and/or jewelry*. These can cause mutual injuries. Spotters may get caught in a swinging chain, and can thus choke the gymnast.

- Wear a *suitable gym outfit*. Large, slippery warm-up suits as well as oversized T-shirts not only make it difficult to do gymnastics, but make it almost impossible for proper grips. Heavy sneakers, as seen in daily life and for sports games, are also not suitable. Not only do they not help the strengthening of the foot in jumps, landings and balancing, but they can also cause severe injuries for the spotters during kick ups to handstand or back hip circles. Barefoot, socks with rubber soles or, best of all, gymnastic shoes are suitable.

- Tie *long hair tightly to the head* for gymnastics. It not only gets in the way during upside down moments, but it's annoying for a spotter to get tangled up in the hair while spotting.

- Obviously *no chewing gum* should be chewed by the gymnast, nor by the spotter.

There are further game rules for team work in order for the gymnasts and the spotters to form a successful team:

- *Before starting* with gymnastics, both sides *need to talk* and *be clear* about which element or sequence of skills will be performed. Questioning is better than to be surprised by negative results.

- Before initiation of the movement, *eye contact* needs to be *established*. That means that the gymnast, too, must watch out for the attention of the spotter before he expects to be helped.

- A harmonious cooperation between spotters and gymnasts can be achieved from the start when the cue is agreed upon. The first swing should always be counted in the direction of movement.

Example:
For the long hang pullover from low bar to high bar, the children swing in preparation up and down with the swinging leg: "1", "2" should occur during the up-swing, finally at "3" when the up-swing to front support on the high bar happens.

• Spotters and gymnasts form a team in order to solve movement problems. Therefore the spotters must be ready to give their full attention, care, good will and empathy for the gymnast for the entire duration of the movement and even beyond that. The gymnasts need to allow themselves to be spotted, and to fully entrust themselves with problems, fears and body to the spotters. Relying on each other can be a wonderful experience.

A teacher/coach must not only be a good technician and intricately know each movement, but should also have good pedagogical and psychological skills. The leading person creates through his own behavior a comfortable, joyful and trusting atmosphere. In case of uncertainly he should always be close by in order to exhibit security.

TRUST

"Children that lack confidence and self-reliance often find retreat in alcohol or drugs. Those who know their strengths know that even difficult situations can be overcome.
Children collect experience. This is where they need the trust of their friends, parents and teacher. The feeling that someone is on their side helps them to withstand difficult situations.
The fear for the well-being of the children makes it, at times, difficult to trust them.
Mutual honesty and openness, especially when something has gone wrong, is a prerequisite for this. Understanding when opinions are contrary is part of it.
Talking with each other can abolish difficulties before a problem may arise.
We can do a lot to prevent children becoming addicted. To trust children is a part of this."

German Center for Health Education
on behalf of the German Ministry of Health

II. Pedagogical, Psychological and Sociological Aspects

1 Children Spot and Secure Each Other

1.1 Motivated and Fear-free Gymnastics

In children's gymnastics different moments of fear can occur:

- Fear of the *new or unknown*. This can refer to new movements, but also to a new apparatus, to unaccustomed heights (balance beam, upper bar of uneven bars), to unsurveyable situations and in a few cases also to spotting.

- Fear *of failure* and *non-achievement*, fear of *shame* in front of the group.

- Fear of *pain* and of *injuries*.

The first person to relate to and trust for overcoming such fears is the teacher.

The following principles are helpful in determining his actions:

The children should

- be cautiously introduced to new apparatus, while including some apparatus information into the lesson and made comfortable with the apparatus through games.

- get to know new skills through selected preparatory exercises. The teacher/coach should if necessary spot at first, and then gradually transfer the job of spotting onto the children themselves.

- experience moments of success through individual suitable tasks – also for spotting. These are experienced especially through mutual support.

- be alerted to situations of risk. The teacher/coach should give reasons, bring insight to the children through talks, and if necessary establish mutually, with the children, rules of conduct that include spotting.

Fig. 18: Working together in small groups

Further people for the children to trust and relate to, are the children in the groups themselves, for example the partner or the small group at the apparatus (Fig. 18). Especially, skilled spotting and securing amongst them creates trust and largely reduces existing fears.

In a climate of trust, encouragement, and allowing oneself be helped, even the weaker students dare to approach more difficult tasks without being fearful of shame. The subjective feeling of well-being in the learning group is an important foundation for fear-free children's gymnastics. That is why mutual spotting amongst the children contributes substantially. Children overcome their fears gradually.

Example:
Many children show fear when kicking up to a handstand. When they are standing upside down they do not know where they are or what to do. They believe that when kicking up to the vertical they do not have control over their body anymore and might fall over and get hurt. Along with this goes the fear of being laughed at in case of failure. For these reasons some children refuse to practice at all. But when these children experience a handstand against the wall, and fellow students can carry and hold them in balance, with skilled spotter grips and verbal encouragement, the kicking to a handstand leads to success and self confidence, and the belief in one's own abilities grows increasingly. Other exercises are then approached with much more courage.

1.2   Social Field of Action

Even though gymnastics is thought of as an individualistic sport, it offers –
and here especially in children's gymnastics – a field of action that is built
upon contact and cooperation abilities. Spotting of the children amongst
themselves starts with a seemingly banal foundation, to want to touch others
and to allow themselves to be touched by others. In school and at the gym
club, on playgrounds and everywhere else in the unrestricted movement life
of the children this "unrestricted cooperation" is no longer present.

First the children are introduced to partners and then to a small group
through small tasks (p. 72 ff.), without yet spotting and securing. For
example at an apparatus station. Only when foundations for cooperation
have been created, can small group work be undertaken through spotting
and securing with group gymnastics, in which everybody is adequately
involved in the learning process.

2   Attitude

The use of spotters requires a positive attitude for assisting and a principal
readiness to help. The readiness for such a "serving" activity expresses itself
in a specific sort of attentiveness and a feeling for responsibility. For many
this ability must first be acquired. How this can be brought
about, in games and a in child-like fashion, is described in the chapter
"Teaching and learning" (p. 71-129). Also conversations about sense and
purpose of spotting and securing give insight for doing this. Only when the
teacher can expect this from his students, can many exercises that include
mutual spotting be possible.

Example:
When rolling forward out of a handstand the spotters must carry the
gymnast into the rolling movement (Fig. 130.2, p. 170). Letting the weak
student drop to his neck from the handstand position would lead to injuries.
It may even occur that children find it funny when another child is being
dropped on purpose. Such groups need to be taught social fundamental
rules through the most simple movements. Acting responsibly is taught
through simple partner exercises. Tension exercises in which children are

lifted by their feet like a stiff board out of a back laying position are first activities that allow the teacher to check for a positive attitude for spotting, and if the child can be trusted.

For newly learned and practiced skills the spotter or securer must assume full responsibility for the gymnast. Many spotter tasks require social maturity. The understanding grows that children should also spot, because, amongst other reasons, if they want to be successful themselves, they must also depend upon assistance. In reverse, the gymnast learns to rely upon the spotters.

Again, readiness needs to exist to allow oneself to be spotted. Many children demonstrate an attitude – at first unaware: "Whoever needs help is weak." To experience assistance as positive is, therefore, one of the most beneficial experiences for the assisting child. Numerous other social abilities and forms of behavior are required for well-functioning work and assistance in small groups, which are also taught at the same time.

3   Commuunication and Cooperation Abilities

To work something out as a team requires at least a *minimum of communication and interaction ability*. These two improve through common action. One feels that a good result is more likely to occur, if everyone contributes his ideas and suggestions. In this regard, the advantage of the small group is also that the shy ones will come forward to say something or demonstrate.

When children assist each other, there is always *intense communication*. They encourage each other, confer with each other, cheer for each other's success, praise and console. Mistakes are attempted to be corrected, tips given on one's own "special" situation, and appropriate spotter actions are experimented with. Only through communication can cooperation grow. Also, the tactile communication of touching each other when spotting, and the non-verbal communication during eye contact before the start of an exercise, are essentials of mutual assistance, not to mention the body language that is being perceived through close partner cooperation.

Fear and courage, joy and exasperation, anger and contentment are experienced through the gymnast's verbal utterances and behavioural forms. Spotters must adapt to this when spotting (see section "Adaptation to the partner", p. 82-84).

The *ability to cooperate* is needed when practice is planned in small groups at various stations with mutual spotting. For unrestricted (open) tasks in newer didactic approaches in gymnastics; for creative, constructive gymnastics and in group gymnastics, different problems are solved independently by the group. If spotting has been introduced in previous learning units, then this knowledge becomes enriched. Tricks can be tried that only work in cooperation with other children, in a small group, through mutual spotting and securing.

Common practice is always confronted with personal, social and subject oriented problems that must be solved without the teacher. One doesn't really help, but always wants to play, another doesn't want to help set up the equipment, a third one cuts in line continuously, and a fourth one needs an answer as to why his pullover doesn't work. *Conflicts and problems* must be *solved with them*. If the organization has been established in such a way that the children help themselves, then they need to deal with these happenings directly and independently.

4   Self-acting and Self-sufficiency

Working in small groups increases the ability *to act for oneself*. For example, it has been observed that before the start of a lesson, children have set up a few mats in order to "quickly" practice handstand forward roll in groups of three. Outside on the school's playground, before class, one observes children practicing pullovers with spotters.

Guidance to self-sufficiency is a declared goal for sport lessons in school. With the early confrontation spotter tasks will children feel a little bit more grown up. They are even proud to work on something independently in a small group. Older children are finally capable through consistent gymnastics and spotting in small groups to set up equipment, warm-up on their own, to practice or to solve a task creatively and to assist and correct each other, mostly independently from the teacher.

5 We-feeling

When a lot of mutual spotting and securing in small groups is employed in practice, one can observe the build-up of *a feeling of togetherness*. Through social proximity the children learn to get to know each other better, to lose their shyness and not be prejudiced. The "we-feeling" grows with every lesson. If the group is allowed to demonstrate something that succeeded, this "we-awareness" atmosphere can be well observed.

This development can particularly be observed by the teacher in newly formed groups of advanced age. If the teacher wants to separate groups after some time, for whatever reason, he meets strong resistance by the members of the groups.

Mutual spotting and securing contributes to the integration of outsiders and weak students. They find their place and acknowledgment in such groups more quickly than in large groups. The one who, for example, cannot make it over the high box or bar, because he is overweight, finds alternatively his proof of ability as a strong spotter, and is appreciated as a group member. Assistance as a part of learning and practicing skills for all, does not single out the weak ones as the sole dependents for assistance.

"Children spotting each other" involves the entire group in common activities, where everybody can find his place.

III. Instructional Aspects

1 INSTRUCTORS IN GYMNASTICS

The introduction to spotting and securing for children is, at first, often a difficult task for the teacher. This counts especially for all groups that are newly formed, and for class and club groups that are only used to being spotted by their teacher or coach. The teacher has to lead the children methodically, systematically and in a long term build up toward the field of spotting, and introduce them to specific abilities.

1.1 Spotting and Securing Performed by Children

Nevertheless, after the often difficult initiation phase, matters become a whole lot easier for the teacher in his instruction. He is no longer the sole spotter or securer. This task can now be delegated and frees him for other tasks.

This leads to *more movement-intensified lessons* for the children. Simultaneous practice is now possible at various apparatus stations; more frequent attempts at skills or exercises are the result.

This further enables lessons, according to the *principle of inner differentiation*. Therefore children can be taught more intensely, and also according to their abilities and attitude.

Examples:
Weaker students practice the handstand with two spotters, stronger students only with one, very strong ones practice handstand forward roll with one safety spotter.

When various apparatus stations are set up, the children may choose their favorite event, if self-organized small group work, including the organization of spotting, has been accomplished prior to this. This not only favors different interests, but the varied, difficult tasks contribute, through the principle of best adaptation, to motivation in gymnastics lessons.

1.2 Care and Supervision Duties

The aspects mentioned so far can only be realized if the teacher acts responsibly with the children, and if he offers his instruction in such a fashion that nothing happens to them. The care and supervision duties demand from the teacher the prevention of accidents, while simultaneously carrying out his pedagogical tasks. The children's education toward independent activity must not jeopardize the safety in school sports.

For example, the guidelines in North-Rhine-Westfalia (one of Germany's states) ask the teacher "to awaken the safety awareness of the students through meaningful guidance and to accustom them to an orderly, circumspect and self-responsible behavior".

> The assignment of same-aged children as spotters is always legitimized, when
> - the chosen tasks are appropriate for the child's abilities
> - the chosen tasks comply with the social degree of maturity of the children
> - a systematic preparation and introduction of spotting and securing preceded the application.

Nevertheless it will also be necessary for the teacher to consequently observe the lesson proceedings, and wherever the situation requires, to act in a helping manner. This can be the case for timid students or for exercises with particularly hazardous moments (Fig. 20).

Teachers act responsibly, with regard to their supervision duties, when children are kept from trying to master an apparatus circuit, only to do those exercises that are easy, and kept from being done without spotting. It's important to point out what is not allowed to be attempted in certain stations.

A teacher acts carelessly, when he allows the children to try anything they want on *mini-tramp or vault without restrictions*. Even when, prior to that, mutual spotting had been worked on, the self-conscious and wild boys or girls often start to do flips off the box or the mini-tramp. This "roll without hands" can often lead to very close head contact with the apparatus, and can cause the knees to hit the face when landing. The spotters are, in this case, over-burdened.

Fig. 19:
Teacher as
a spotter

Fig. 20:
Building a
"spotter team"
with the
teacher

The latter also applies to situations where the *relationship between spotter and apparatus no longer fits.* When practicing a straddle vault over a long horse the spotters are hopelessly over-burdened, despite having learned how to use the support grip, when the apparatus (as a measure of differentiation for stronger students), in the course of practice, is over head height (Fig. 19). The spotters can't reach for the arms anymore. In this case the teacher must take over the spotting task (Fig. 19, 20).

The spotters must receive *a methodical introduction* for the required activity from the teacher, or must be given information and clear instructions for the start of spotting.

It's also careless to allow children to swing without restrictions on the swinging rings, without any methodical introduction and restrictive hints. While absorbed in the thrill of a movement, those children that have not learned the proper technique, release their grip at the wrong moment and do not land correctly. A readily positioned spotter is in any case helpless, when trying to prevent a fall.

The teacher who offers or requests unrestricted gymnastics on apparatus that mislead to dare-devil actions, who positions children to spot dynamic movements without instruction, and then even leaves the scene unsupervised, is acting very carelessly in children's gymnastics. This unfortunately is more common than one would like to think.

2 Method – Learning Paths for Qualified Spotting, Accompanying and Securing: Explanations

In order to acquire spotting abilities, learning processes are necessary that need to be steered according to plan. Thus, the achievement of competence

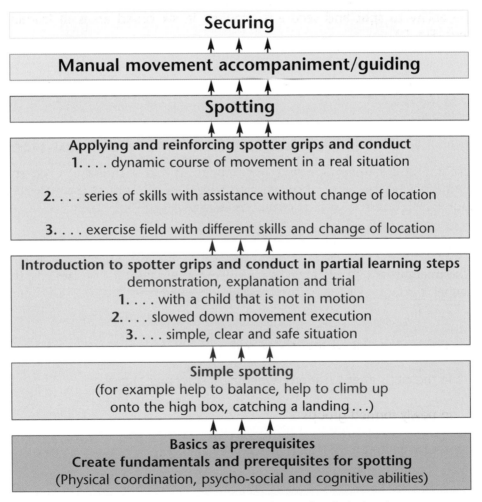

Fig. D: Steps of introduction to qualified spotting/manual technical assistance

for qualified assistance becomes a matter of instruction. Methodical steps are necessary, just like in gymnastics, when learning a new skill. Klaus Hermann, one of the few who many years ago published a book on spotting and securing writes: "One can't expect from any student that, through a one time explanation of the raw skill of spotting, he will succeed with regard to the aforementioned skills, let alone have him understand how to apply the technique appropriately. It requires lots of patience, knowledge and methodically correct and thorough procedures for passing on such information." (Hermann 1978). The ability to spot and secure is acquired in six broad areas of learning steps (Fig. D).

EXPLANATIONS

2.1   First Level: Fundamentals and Prerequisites

Teaching and learning spotting, accompanying and securing in children's gymnastics begins with a first learning level, the creating of prerequisites, upon which good, qualified spotting is based.

Longterm Fundamental Work

Fundamentals for an effective, supportive cooperation are created by the teacher through playful partner and group tasks (see practical examples, p. 72-129)

•   at the beginning of the school year

•   in the clubs after vacations, when new enrollment starts

•   in newly formed groups

•   in groups that have been taken over

It's these different forms of activities for the improvement of contact and cooperation abilities that are, amongst others, regarded as prerequisites for the actual spotting and securing. The children learn in a playful manner with single, partner and group tasks to:

- at first, *establish eye and body contacts*

- *awaken attention* and *reaction abilities*

- *adapt* to *partners* and *their movements*

- *get used* to the *partner's body weight*

- develop *responsibility* and *trust* through the interaction with others

(See practical examples in the practice section, p. 72-104)

Creating Prerequisites Before the Start of the Lesson

When *the lessons begin* there should be preparatory exercises and game types with emphasis on cooperative ability, adaptability and reaction ability. This is part of the introductory instruction program, *in order to warm up for the following spotter tasks*, which means for *work with a partner or in a group* and *for situation appropriate actions in gymnastics*. Certain tasks have shown to be advantageous that are posed in a context of "criss-cross running in the gym". From the beginning of the lesson and throughout this requires a degree of attention and alertness that is needed during spotting, because, when running through the gym in an unrestricted manner, the students have to watch out, in order to avoid collisions. Additional posing of tasks (for example include running leaps when running) increase these demands. Reaction tasks, during warm-up running, awaken alertness and readiness for the following spotter tasks.

Partner exercises during preparatory stretching can also prepare for mutual acceptance (see also further suggestions in the following chapter about practice examples, p. 72-129).

At the beginning of the main lesson simple spotter tasks should be used during warm-up, in order to get accustomed to them. Time for repetitive attempts should be given often. Principally, the movements should be well supported, before they are finally secured.

2.2 Second Level: Learning Simple Spotting

At the second level, easy spotter actions are added.

Examples:

- Balance assistance is given through hand reaching while walking on a beam or any other balancing activity (Fig. 21).

- Grip securing is given through reaching around the wrists when hanging in tuck hang, while swinging and flipping forward or backwards on the rings, high bar or uneven bars (Fig. 178a/b, p. 201).

Fig. 21: Balance assistance

- Jumps off boxes, or vaults from the end of the beam, or the landing after underswing movements, are caught at the stomach and back through "forking" (Fig. 120, 121, 122, p. 162-163).

2.3 Third and Fourth Level: Spotter Grips and Actions

Introduction to Spotter Grips

A third learning level leads on from the second, one of the systematic introductions to spotter grips. The technique for certain spotter grips:

- is first *demonstrated* by the teacher on a *non-moving* child

- is then *tried* as a grip on a non-moving child, and, if necessary, corrected by the teacher.

Example:

- Teacher checks for thumbs reaching around the upper arm in support grip, or if the pointer finger is laid on, if the inner hand supports sufficiently underneath the armpit, or in the elbow area (which would be incorrect).

- Hereafter the technique *is tried* in *simple, surveyable situations.*

Examples:

- Spotters lift a jumper with support grip at the upper arms, or assist the down jump from a box.

- The grip onset for a handstand against the wall is tested when a support grip at the thighs is applied, where the gymnast gets moved away from and back to the wall (Fig. 101, p. 142).

- The spotting child turns the gymnast with a forward turn grip in such a way that the gymnast bows forward.

Application of the Techniques

Following this the new technique is applied at the fourth level in *hazard free* situations, while still executing the movement *slowly.*

Examples:

- For the support grip at the upper arms the children squat onto a box, the spotters reach around the upper arms and carry the gymnast off the box. The situation is increasingly accelerated.

During the support grip at the thigh for the handstand the gymnast boldly pushes out of the wall handstand into the vertical. The spotter quickly reaches around the thigh and prevents the gymnast from falling over.

(Also see the practical examples for approaches within a lesson unit in the section about practice, p. 141-163)

Learning How to Execute Complex Spotter Actions

With increasing dynamics of the gymnastics movement the spotters need to be more and more skilled, because further tasks are demanded from the spotter:

- He has to choose his *location* correctly.

- He has to establish *eye contact* with the gymnast and observe from the beginning onward, in order to estimate the movement dynamics and its range. Also, in this phase, fear and dare-devil behaviors

can be observed by the spotters, judged by the look and facial expressions of the gymnast. The intensity and the manner of spotting is "pre-structured".

- He has *to move toward* the gymnast with his hands.

- He has *to apply* the *spotter grip*.

- He has *to accompany* the movement of the gymnast and, if necessary, even *guide it in a correcting way*, but in accordance with the co-spotter (if, for example, one helps too much, the gymnast might get twisted while airborne).

- Finally, he must secure *the landing* of the gymnast.

2.4   Fifth Level: Executing Movement Accompaniment

The more complex the movement is, the more refined spotter skills become.

With increasing the standard of the gymnast, movement support turns more and more into movement accompaniment on behalf of the spotter. It has to be pointed out to the children to support a skill only as far as is necessary in order to succeed. Movement accompaniment as assistance after the principle "as much as necessary, as little as possible" should at first only be tried with single, possibly easy, and with skills that have been almost completely mastered.

Examples:

- Pullover on the bars: The spotting children reach for the gymnast's seat. They accompany the up swinging movement without lifting the body from the beginning. Only when the spotting children recognize that the gymnast can't accomplish it, and might fall back, is the center of gravity pushed up by the seat against the bar.

- Kicking up to handstand: The close spotting hands approach the legs of the gymnast. If the spotters feel that the gymnast's kick was insufficient, or has too much swing and might fall over, they reach to correct and support.

A higher level of assistance finally shows during spotting of skills in movement connections. Constantly, the accompanying hands are by the side of the gymnast's body, without continuously spotting or guiding. Spots are only given in problem situations. Should the gymnast be able to do it on his own, then movement accompaniment turns into securing the course of the movement.

Active movement support and guidance, as well as accompaniment, are finally applied as an area in movement connections with newly learned and achieved skills. Highest demands are posed for spotting children when, within a movement connection, different spotter grips have to be used, locations need to be changed, and if there are changes from spotting to accompanying.

Example for an accompanying movement connection

- Pull-over (known skill) ⟶ movement accompaniment

- Back hip circle ⟶ movement steering
  (newly learned skill)

- Cast and second back hip circle ⟶ same spotter grip,
  (the 'new' skills in series)   applied twice in a row

- Jump down and under swing ⟶ change of location and landing
  (known skills)   security

This situation should be posed as an exercise task for advanced children. They not only improve their spotting abilities, but also prepare these skills for securing abilities. The teacher can finally also recognize how far these spotter grips and actions have become automated and absorbed.

2.5   Sixth Level: Ability to Secure

At last the children are able to secure those skills that they previously spotted and accompanied. But the teacher has to constantly point out that:

*   the course of the movement must be *attentively* observed

*   *hands* and *body* need *to be ready*

*   in case of an incorrect movement *nobody jumps away*, but quickly approaches the gymnast in order to reach in supportively.

All learning levels that help acquire spotter abilities are demonstrated in the following examples.

B PRACTICE ... FOR CONSULTATION

I. Teaching and Learning

The following practical suggestions refer to the step-by-step approach from the ability to spot until the ability to secure (commonly known as safety spotting), as was described in section A III. 2, p. 62-69. At first, as a fundamental for spotting in gymnastics, numerous game and exercise suggestions *for the improvement of cooperation* are shown. The second step shows tasks for learning *simple spotting* during gymnastics practice. A third step demonstrates, in using two examples, *how spotting until securing* can be *learned step by step* in the gymnastics group. In the last chapter of the practice section *the spotter grips* of the skills are structured according to apparatus groups.

1 First Step: Creation of Basics and Prerequisites

In interaction pedagogy games take on a central role. Basic qualifications of the cooperative and the social-togetherness behavior can be learned in a playful way. Through agreements (rules), the children's play becomes structured. Literature though primarily mentions games in which competitiveness takes on a more important role, instead of cooperative behavior. Rarely can one find interactive games that propagate "give and take". Cooperation means standing by a friend, keeping agreements, caring for others, the group cohesiveness, without going against somebody or another group.

In this section of the book exercise and game types have been collected that promote cooperation. Starting with getting to know each other and establishing contacts, adapting to partners and their movements, getting used to their body weight, taking on responsibility and having confidence, learning to communicate and initiating cooperation, all the way to exercise

games from partner and group acrobatics (where all abilities come together), without yet using gymnastics apparatus, all fundamentals for the cooperation are created.

The awakening of attention and reaction games are helpful for execution of such playful tasks at the beginning of the lesson. For this reason there are also examples given for this. The choice of the game types serves for a better overview for which focal points can be placed. According to problems that a teacher or coach may encounter in class, he can quickly find exercises for these. If, for example, there is difficulty in children not wanting to touch each other, the teacher can find game types under the heading "body contact", that he may include in the lesson plan at the beginning. A large part of the following exercises is multi-functional.

1.1 More than 100 Games and Exercise Forms for Encouraging Cooperation

Age Sections and Game Types

Almost all of the following game types are appropriate starting at five years old, and, depending on the tasks, all the way up to youth and adulthood. A rough age orientation for the selection of the game types can be described as follows:

Clear, *with easy game rules* briefly explained, games give *pre-school children* (ages 4-6) the security to get into the game. *Two-some games* are preferred for practicing cooperation. With the beginning of school, traditional games are well liked. *Elementary school children* (7-10 years old) begin to learn *cooperation in groups*. Stiff rules gain more and more acceptance, and their sense for fairplay demands the keeping of the rules in often verbally loud ways. At approximately age 9, *social games* become well liked. The social component, the experience of the *"we-feeling"*, becomes established which continues through to the *teenage years*. But they also demand tasks that allow for *creative involvement* of the participants through their ability to invent.

The following exercises serve well for the warm-up phase of the starting lesson through tasks that are associated with running.

Getting to Know Each Other and Contact Games

With easy game types, especially for newly formed groups or classes, the first inter-human relations can be formed and prejudice (through speech or way of dressing) be eliminated. If the game itself already furthers the initiation of contact (this is how children act in their unrestricted movement life), there are also special games for getting to know each other, from which all profit with regard to their mutual actions in the lessons to come. Getting to know each other is the starting point for being able to help each other.

Learning names: This spot next to me is empty . . .

This introductory form is especially advisable for the youngest. The children sit in small circles. There is a gap between two children. Now the first child hits the floor with the hand next to him and says: "The spot next to me is empty, I wish for . . . (child's name) . . . to come here". The children have to remember each other's names. It's also a good opportunity for the teacher to learn the names of these new classmates. Hint: If one child is called too often the teacher should step in and regulate this.

Finding friends

The children are running (possibly accompanied by music) through the gym. Upon an earlier agreed signal (clap of hands, call or music stop), every child looks for a partner with whom he continues to run. With the next signal they separate. The children continue to run alone until the next signal from the teacher.

Variations:

- The children count along, how many friends were they able to find?
- The children make sounds when forced to separate, like sobbing, "oooh"-calls, "Bye-bye!".
- The children run right away to somebody else when separating.
- The game can be connected with the following contact games.

Icebreaker: Greeting games

The children run (possibly accompanied by music) through the gym. Upon an earlier agreed signal (clap of hands, call or music stop) every child looks for a partner and they greet each other individually. They may shake hands for example and say: "Well how are you doing?".

Music: Popular pieces of music that contain the greeting as chorus ("Good morning...").

Variations:

- Greeting each other like fellow students.

- Greeting each other like old friends.

- Introducing oneself during the greeting and when, accidentally, or announced by the teacher, they find they are back with each other, they must mention the name again ("Your name was...?!").

International Greetings

- To greet like Chinese (hands held together in front of chin and bow)

- To greet like Australians by lifting one hand and saying "Hey!".

- To greet like Texans (Hand shake, the other hand claps on the shoulder and say: "Hey Y'all" or "Howdy partner"!)

The following suggestions assume a certain maturity.

- To greet like Russians (hug and say "brother/sister").

- To greet like Italian friends (reach around the shoulders and give air kisses onto the left and right cheeks along with a "Ciao") or like French relatives (three air kisses on the right, left, right with a "Salut").

- To greet like Eskimos (rub noses from right to left).

- Ask for ideas from the participants for other international greeting forms.

Athlete greetings

- To greet like two old gym friends (run toward each other and hug).

- To greet like Equestrians by tipping their hat.

- To greet like basketball players with high fives.

- To celebrate like volleyball players (jump up and clap hands over head).

- To celebrate like soccer players after a goal.

- To greet before practice like in Judo (Sit on heels, hands lie on the floor in front of the knees and bow with the forehead to the floor).

- How are the handball players doing it? Hockey players, skate boarders...?

Special greetings

- Curtsey in front of a king.

- A gentleman tips his hat in front of a lady, she performs a curtsey and lowers the head.

- A gentleman gives an allusion of a handkiss, she nods her head.

- Like in the old times, girls do a curtsey, boys bow.

Eye Contact

To blink and squint

The children are positioned in pairs in a circle one step away from each other. The ones in front form an inner circle, the ones in the back with their hands held behind the back, form an outer circle. One child stands alone in the outer circle and blinks someone over with his eyes from the inner circle. The one blinked at quickly runs over to the new outside partner, the former partner tries to quickly keep him from running away.

Hints:

- When groups are large, two or more double circles should be formed.

- If the group number is even, one child becomes the "joker" and is exchanged when the attempt to blink somebody over fails three times.

Contact search

The first task is: Out on a run, try to establish eye contact with a partner. Each time during the run the children should look for another child, while a child looks for the eye contact with someone else. The one with mutual eye contact then runs towards the other, and greets through head bowing. When they pass each other slowly, the contact initiation is finished and they start looking for a new partner.

In the next run through, further tasks are posed after the "viewing" of a partner, where eye contact should be kept continuously.

Round-about and clear in view

The children run around free and establish eye contact with another child. After that they walk or run once around each other while keeping eye contact. The ones who do not look away demonstrate that they are not afraid. After one round they say good-bye to each other and nod their head. Again, they keep running criss-cross through the gym until a new eye contact is established, or until they are "hit" by another requesting look of another child; repeat the running around each other.

Variation:

- After this the children run once around each other without changing the front (this means at first right shouldered, then back to back and left shouldered, back to the starting point). They keep long eye contact and look for it quickly again.

Body Contact

The following game types usually begin with free running in order to guarantee movement intensity of the lesson, and to achieve random groupings. Through the quick and spontaneous forming of the groups, the children often forget about their fear of being touched. Upon the call of the teacher and out of the run, the children establish eye contact with someone close by. Thereupon, both are to fulfill a task together. At first these tasks should carefully prepare for the mutual touching and taking hold of each other. As a warm-up exercise it's advised to begin with "find a friend" (see above).

Dance

The different forms of classic and modern youth dances are very good for finding each other. Dancing with each other incorporates many forms for social contact initiation, like adapting to a partner, communication, mutual acting and body contact. Thus, hands are reached for in the circle format for the "polonaise", hands are placed on the shoulders and around the hips, or for an illustrative dance they communicate with each other. Dancing examples are so numerous that we cannot include them all here.

Open, free dancing to music should be used as an initiation for which, as an orientation, the dance actions can be derived from the lyrics of the song. Hereafter, simple playful forms are given that can be used for the beginning of the lesson. It's suggested to use "running music" with 168 beats per minute (for example rock n' roll music), or music to bounce to, like the "Sabre Dance".

Run toward each other and, while walking, running and bouncing around, continue to move with easy hand grasping.
- Try different hand grips at different heights.

- Hook in elbows and continue to move.

Variations:
- Hook right arm into right arm of someone else and walk, run and bounce around.

- Hook right arm into left arm of someone else and walk, run, bounce forward, sideward and backward.

- Continue to move with over-cross hand grasping; both have the same movement direction ("Ring around the rosy type rhymes"-posture: right hand into the right hand of the partner, left into the left and keep one's own arms in front of one's own body) or

- With over cross hand grasping for the "wind mill" turn around the common center point.

- Continue to move with one arm from the front/back around the hips.

Polonaise Blankenese

Dance a polonaise to music through the gym (see Fig. 22).

Variation:
- Walk over or underneath the equipment that's already set up.

Fig. 22: Polonaise

Newspaper dance
There are as many newspapers lying in the gym as there are children. The children run freely through the gym (best to music) without touching the newspapers. To jump over is allowed (desired). Upon the call "pause" or music stop, the children have to stand as quickly as possible on a newspaper. During the ongoing course of the game, more and more newspapers are eliminated so that several children have to stand on one paper.

Siamese twins
Two children stand back to back and have a newspaper squeezed between them. They now try to move, bend down or turn with the paper.

Variation:
- The children dance to the music without losing the paper. Who demonstrates the craziest dance?!

Attention: The owl glues!
In "the owl glues" call of the teacher, the students try to establish eye contact with someone close by and glue as they meet each other. Glued as such, they must try to continue moving around.

Variations:
- The teacher determines certain body parts to be glued together, for example being glued at the shoulders and continuing to move.
- The children run to music. When the music stops they quickly look for a partner and become glued together. The participants should be encouraged to invent further possibilities, where they can become glued together at the seat, forehead, back.

Magnet game
The children walk, step, run, bounce through the gym. Upon the call: "Magnetism!" by the teacher (or a chosen child), the children continue as twos, threes or fours with those close by, like magnets that attract each other and attach to each other.

Variations:
- The children freeze. Whenever a child detaches he receives negative points.

- The teacher calls the name of a body part of which the children need to touch themselves, for example: "Magnet: nose!"

Sculptor

Two children stand together. One child tries as "a sculptor" to create a statue out of his partner, while putting head, arms, legs and trunk into position (Fig. 23).

Fig. 23: Sculptor

Large airplanes

Upon the call of the teacher two or three children quickly find each other and play airplane while running through the gym. The child in front, as the tip of the airplane, reaches with his hands from underneath to the children in the back. Then, they run through the gym with this hand grasping (Fig. 24).

Traffic

A traffic policeman stands elevated on a box in the center of the gym and directs traffic. If he lifts a hand everybody stops, when arms go to the side the traffic flows and more of the similar. The children illustrate cars as twosomes, trucks as threesomes, large trucks as foursomes, and buses as fivesomes. Additionally, they may make typical sounds. At "stop," they become silent or make low idling sounds.

Fig. 24: Large airplanes

Variations:

- The gym equipment can be used as "houses," streets, or valleys and similar ideas.

- To music (for example "Summer in the city"), at music stop everybody freezes as if they have just seen a ghost.

79

Volcano

The children squat tightly together and extend their arms into the middle of the circle. At first the teacher describes the activity of the volcano. The children make noises trying to simulate a volcano eruption. At first the volcano bubbles faintly, then, at times, a flame sizzles out of the volcano center (one arm is extended upward with a sizzling noise) and at last the volcano erupts with a loud bang (all run away or fall to the outside onto the floor).

Gordian knot

Upon call of a number between six and ten, groups start forming that stand very close to each other. Without looking upward, all extend their arms toward the ceiling and reach for a hand until there are no more free hands. Without letting go, the group carefully parts and tries to keep the resultant knot (Fig. 25).

Fig. 25: Gordian knot

Knot father

Six to eight children form a circle with hands held, one child is chosen to be the knot father and stands with his back to the group. Through climbing over or diving underneath the clasped hands, through body twists, without loosening the hand grasp and similar movements, the group knots together in a tight bunch. If no one can move anymore, all call loudly for the knot father. He tries to recreate the original circle by giving instructions (Fig. 26).

Fig. 26: Knot father

Jelly-fish

The children run and bounce freely in space. Upon call of the teacher, they find each other in groups of five to seven in a circle and reach around their backs or shoulders. The jelly-fish now begins to swim (or breathe).

The children all move simultaneously, through lowering of the trunk to the center of the circle and rising again. "Which group finds a regular rhythm first?"

Fig. 27.1-27.2: Jelly-fish

Variation:

*   The jelly-fish is in locomotion: "Which group can move simultaneously in different directions while making the swimming or breathing movements of a jelly-fish?" (Fig. 27.1-27.2)

Sitting serpent

This "group curiosity" is also very much liked by older children. One participant sits on the floor, a bench, a small box or a chair, and supports himself with his hands behind his back. The next child sits now on his knees, the next on the knees of the second one and so forth until a sitting serpent is created.

Variation:

*   A closed circle can be created with this for taller children. An exceptional task is accomplished (if necessary with help from outside), when this sitting circle moves forward.

Snail

Three to six children run slowly as a chain through the gym. The leading child is the snail head. Upon the call of the teacher, the snail (chain) rolls in and around the snail's head. The chain cannot break, otherwise the snail "dies" (Fig. 28.1-28.2).

Fig. 28.1-28.2: Snail

Tree log rolling

All find partners. One child is in prone position on the floor (panel mat), the arms are held next to the body. The partner now rolls the tightened body as a tree log into a back lying position, prone... and back.

Adaptation to the Partner

Good spotting requires the ability to adapt to the movements of the partner. This includes, amongst other things, constant attention, and the ability to concentrate and to observe. The following exercises improve the ability to adapt to a partner and to his movements. Simultaneously communicative situations are offered, in which listening to each other, exactly observing one another, and possibly the tactile senses are trained. The expression of the other, his temperament, his body movements are observed and brought into the game. Miming, gesticulation, posture and demeanor are explored in pantomime and illustrative games. Perception is of great importance for good (in parts non-verbal) communication, and also for mutual spotting.

First Partner Exercises

The children run in pairs together through the gym. Upon call of the teacher, the children perform small movement tasks:

* Partner A straddles the legs, Partner B crawls underneath, then they change and continue to run (Fig. 29).

* Partner A is rolled up, sitting on heels on the floor, partner B jumps over, then they change and continue to run.

Variations:

* Partner B straddles legs after landing and A crawls underneath, then change over and continue to run (Fig. 29).

Fig. 29: Jump over and crawl underneath

- Partner A goes into a bench position, partner B performs a squat wende with support on the shoulder blades or the seat of the kneeling partner.
- Partner B crawls after the landing underneath the bench (Fig. 29).

Elevator

Two children stand back to back and now try, without losing back contact or using their hands, to sit down together on the floor. "Who can stand up again?!" (Fig. 30)

Variation:

- It's simpler to sit on a bench or a box for this exercise.

Fig. 30: Elevator

Mirror picture

The children stand closely in front of each other. The one standing in front of the "mirror" presents movements through miming and gesticulation (making faces also counts), and the mirror must try to imitate it exactly.

Variation:

- Play themes: in the morning when brushing teeth or when dressing, trying on clothes in the store...

Mind puzzle

The teacher asks what does a sad, happy, joyful, angry... face looks like? The children try it out. Then, the children stand in pairs in front of each other and demonstrate their moods. The partner should be able to read the condition from the facial expression.

Variation:

- Include body posture.
- Include body movements.

Newspaper blanket

The children gather in pairs. One child is lying on his back on the floor, the other one covers him with newspapers. Then the child underneath the papers is questioned as to how he feels, if it's dark, if he is afraid, if he could go to sleep . . . After the other child has also been covered with papers, and the pair groupings in the class have been changed, the teacher should lead a discussion where all exchange experiences.

Adapting to Movements

Big tree stem rolls

Two children lie, holding hands, in prone position facing each other. Upon a signal that they agreed upon beforehand (also non-verbal), they now roll as tree stems in a certain direction and back.

Variation:

- It's a lot of fun for the smaller children to start the rolling from inclines.

Copy machine

a   b

Fig. 31a/b: Copy machine

The movements of the partner are "copied." In one location they should at first execute

- only arm movements

- trunk and head movements

- only leg movements

- total body movements

Hereafter, tasks to "copy"

- can be posed in a sideward, forward or backward movement.

Fig. 32: Copy in movement

Hint:

The teacher can demonstrate the movement in front of the group as an introduction, whereupon all children try to copy the movement simultaneously.

Variations:

*   Alternately the children can replace the teacher and, in front of all, demonstrate movement executions.

*   Tasks in twos or threes should follow in order to support the cooperation.

Freeze

The children run in pairs through the gym. Upon call "A", partner A freezes, partner B tries to copy the frozen figure. Best frozen figures receive bonus points (Fig. 33).

Fig. 33: Freeze

Echo

A child slowly changes his body posture, the partner tries to copy the demonstrated movement with the same speed, only slightly delayed (Fig. 34.1-34.2).

Variation:

*   Partner A performs a movement sequence that can become longer. Partner B tries to copy it entirely, at the exact same time.

Fig. 34.1-34.2: Echo

Shadow

The partners stand behind each other and try to copy the movements at the same time.

The movements should be done slowly at first (Fig. 35.1-35.2).

Fig. 35.1-35.2: Shadow

Variations:

*   The shadow lies flat on the floor. "Who can still be a good shadow?" The movements should be executable for the one lying on the floor and be done very slowly at first.
*   Imagine the summer sun is standing in its zenith at noon. There is hardly a shadow to be seen on the floor. You have to stand really close to your partner and copy the movements.

Shadow run

A child runs or hops around and decides upon body movements and movement directions (Fig. 36a). One to two children try to copy the demonstrator quickly (Fig. 36b).

Hint:

This exercise format serves to sharpen vigilance and trains reaction ability.

Fig. 36a/b: Shadow run

Mirror picture in the fitness/ballet studio

The partners are facing each other. Partner A demonstrates a body movement in standing position, Partner B tries to copy it mirror like almost simultaneously (Fig. 37.1-37.2).

Variation:

- Include sideward, forward and backward movements.

Fig. 37.1-37.2: Mirror

Dominoes

Three to six children position themselves in a row and hold their arms up. The child standing in front imitates the "falling of a domino stone" through his arms and side swaying of the upper body. The children behind try, one after another, to copy this movement (Fig. 38.1-38.3).

Variation:

- Two rows stand facing each other and try to execute the movements mirror like.

Fig. 38.1-38.3: Dominoes

Waddle duck run

Two to five children stand very close, next to each other, hook in and bend their knees. Now, they "waddle" (walk) as quickly as possible together over a certain distance (10-30 feet, or the length of a volleyball field line).

Wobble run line

Two or more children stand with straddled legs in a row, behind each other and reach between their legs for one hand (the right hand to the front, the left between their own legs reaches back) (Fig. 39). "Try to walk through the gym with the same rhythm."

Fig. 39: Wobble run line

Variations:

* Run, hop, limp and movement sequences.

* Slalom run/obstacle course over benches, mats and underneath bars.

* Wobble dance to music.

Centipede

The children squat down behind each other and reach for the ankles of the one in front. The centipede slowly starts to move forward; hands are not supposed to be loosened! (Fig. 40).

Fig. 40: Centipede

Getting Acquainted with the Body Weight

The following exercises help the children to become familiar with the body weight of the partner.

Scale

Two children stand on one leg, closely in front of each other, and reach for each other's wrists. Now, both lean back at the same time and try to find their balance in that position. Without loosening the grip, different positions/body postures are tested, for example spreading the working leg to the side or tucking it up (Fig. 41)

Fig. 41: Scale

Pull fight

Two children stand facing each other in relation to a marking (or on a mat) and reach for their hands. Upon a signal they try to pull the partner over the marking (line or mat). Thereafter the winners of the neighboring groups pull-fight against each other, the "second ones" against the "second ones" of the other groups and so forth (Fig. 42).

Fig. 42: Pull fight

Japanese Sumo fight (push fight)

Two children stand on one or four mats (a square area), or they stand facing each other over a line. They lift their arms and put their hands together. Upon call a they try to push each other from the mat or over the line (Fig. 43.1-43.2).

Fig. 43.1-43.2: Japanese Sumo fight

Limp run

Two to three partners stand behind each other, the first one (if three, also the second one) lifts his foot, so the second (third) can reach for it. Which group is able to move like this through half of the gym?" (Fig. 44)

Fig. 44: Limp run

Five leg run

The children position next to each other in threes. The outer ones reach for their inner hand, the middle one puts his arms on the shoulders of the partners and puts one leg onto the grasped hands. "Can you make it to the middle of the gym without loosening the grip?"

First Aid transport

Three children with similar weight form a group. Two create a sitting surface with their hands (the left hand reaches around one's own right wrist, the right hand reaches around the left wrist of the partner) (Fig. 45a). The third partner sits on top of the hands and is carried through the gym for a few steps (Fig. 45b).

Hint:

The spotters cannot start the lift with an arched back, but they must tighten their tummy muscles ("pull in stomach"). They should stand up through straightening of the knees.

Fig. 45 a/b: First Aid transport

Hanging bridge

The children group in pairs. They stand facing each other and reach with their hands to form a tight connection (the left hand grasps their own right wrist, the right hand grasps the left wrist of the partner). With this hand

grasp, the pairs stand shoulder to shoulder, tightly next to each other to form a lane. One child mounts on top of the lane by starting to support himself on the shoulders of the first two pairs (if necessary with the help of the teacher). While maintaining his balance through holding on to the heads of the standing ones, the child now tries to walk all the way through the lane (Fig. 46).

Variation:

• Five pairs and a lighter child form a group. As soon as he passes the first pair, they release their hand grasp and run to the end of the lane, in order to create a new step surface for the walking child. The other pairs act in like fashion.

Fig. 46: Hanging bridge

Wheel barrel

The children get together in pairs. One child is in prone position and supports with his hands next to the shoulders, tightens the body ("pull stomach in") and lifts into a push-up position with straddled legs. The second child stands between the legs and lifts the child into horizontal push-up position, holding on to *the knees* and reaching around the *thighs*. For the advanced, partner stays at the feet (Fig. 47).

Fig. 47: Wheel barrel

Now they walk together forward, backward or in circles.

Variation for the advanced partner:

Wheel barrel in a reverse position (Fig. 48.1-48.2).

Fig. 48.1-48.2: Wheel barrel in reverse position

Fig. 49.1-49.3

Variations:

- Frontal push-up (partner lifts by the feet with legs together) (see Fig. 47).

- Reverse push-up position (with straddled or closed legs) (see Fig. 48.1-48.2).

- Frontal push-up, reverse or sideward in conjunction with longitudinal turns (for the advanced, partner keeps turning at the feet) (Fig. 49.1-49.3).

Board lifts

Exercise for complete body closure: The practicing child goes into a back lying position and tightens all muscles

("stiff man"). The supporting partner squats down, close to the feet, and starts lifting the partner with a straight back ("squeeze your buttocks, stomach to the ceiling") (Fig. 50).

Fig. 50

Variation:

- The lifter only reaches for one leg, but the exercise should be executed in the exact same way.

Putting-up the breakfast board

A group of four gets together on a mat. One child is lying on his back on the mat, arms held close to the body. One partner stands by the head and reaches underneath the head. The other two

Fig. 51

stand next to the shoulders and reach around the upper arms, close to the armpit (Fig. 51): "Wait until the lying partner is a stiff man and lift him into a stand!"

Variation:

- For older and more disciplined children, the lifted child gets to be put back into the back lying position without bending at the hips. The exercise can be done on a soft mat (mat) (Fig. 52).

Fig. 52: Breakfast board

Conveyer belt

Six to ten older children move into a straddle, sit closely together and lift their arms up high. One child lies stiff like a board with the stomach side on top of their hands. The sitting children now try to transport the lying child, with their hands, over head to the other end. Arriving at the end the transported child supports himself on the floor and climbs back to his feet or rolls off (Fig. 53).

Fig. 53: Conveyer belt

Flying fish

The children position themselves in pairs facing each other, forming a lane and grasping each others wrists. One child lies stiff like a board, with the stomach on top of the grasped hands. The "fish" gets transported to the other end by being thrown in the air and getting caught again. At the end the fish glides from a motionless position with a forward roll onto a mat.

Responsibility and Trust

Small tasks can help develop an awareness for responsibility and trust for spotting, and allowing one's self to be spotted.

Test to keep still

All find partners. One is lying on his back on the floor with arms extended. The partner walks, runs, jumps (depending on age) over legs and arms, in a circular pattern over the partner.

Variations:

• Jump diagonally over the lying body.

• Jump over the head and keep eyes open.

• Jump over the wide spread arms and the straddled legs, circling around the trunk.

• Find a rhythm when jumping (see above).

• Jump over arms and legs on one leg for one round.

Obstacle jumping

Children are in groups of twos or threes. They try different positions, like lying on their side, bench, hunched sitting on heels, or a scissors sit with widely spread arms, and allow themselves to be jumped over (Fig. 54).

Courageous stick dance from Bali

Three to four children form a group. Two of them kneel down facing each other at a rod's (broom stick) length. In each hand they hold a stick which is also held by the opposite partner. Now

Fig. 54: Obstacle jumping

they beat and move the sticks together and apart again. One child jumps from outside quickly between the stick lane when it is open, and quickly back out. If there is a fourth child in the group, he jumps next, when the sticks opens up again.

The "dancers" must try to jump faster and faster in and out. One could create a performance to music.

Hint:

The stick beater must find a calm, regular rhythm. This should be practiced before the jumping between the sticks starts.

Exercises with Eyes Closed

Tasks that prove trust are, amongst others, walking movement tasks, for which the eyes remain closed. The exercises become more exciting when using a scarf or bandana to cover the eyes.

In the dark

For this game children stand in a circle, with one child in the center, having his eyes blindfolded (with a bandana or scarf). The blindfolded child tries to catch a player, and through touching, guesses who it is. The one who has been guessed right becomes the next blindfolded person.

Blindfolded man with escort

The children walk in pairs through the gym. One is the blindfolded, the other the escort. Through hand holding and announcing directions the blindfolded can be guided (Fig. 55).

Variations:

• Slalom around set-up apparatus.

• "Over stick and stone": Obstacle walk over mats, benches ... (see photo page 70)

Fig. 55: Blindfolded man

Themes are given: "Guide your blindfolded partner through the supermarket, forest, main street ..., tell the partner what you just saw, where you are walking now."

Seeing eye dog with partner

The children walk in pairs through the gym. One is blindfolded and the other is his seeing eye dog. The dog pulls his master with a gymnastics stick to the goal.

Steer me!

The escort remains behind the blindfolded partner and steers the movement wordlessly through gentle pushing of the right or left shoulder of the blindfolded: "Who can bring his partner safely over to the other side?"

Guide me!

The blindfolded walks without any bodily touching to a designated point. The escort gives verbal instructions.

Field day for the blind

Without a personal escort half of the group goes with eyes covered to a designated line or place. The remaining observing half sees to it that they arrive safely.

Target walk with blindfolded eyes

A line that runs across the gym is the designated target. Four to five groups need to be formed. One child per group is sent out blindfolded for a walk. When the blindfolded believes he has reached the line, he stops. The one who stands closest to the line receives a team point. The other group members pay attention so that nobody walks into the wall.

Sleep chain

All walk slowly across the floor with eyes closed. When meeting someone else they hold hands and continue together. When more than four chain members have come together they split up again.

Carry Exercises

For the following exercises the gymnast learns that his body weight can be carried by partners. The proof of trust is given through maintaining good body tension throughout, and by not supporting himself with one foot backward underneath the body. On the other side, the spotters need to handle the passive gymnast with responsibility, in order to establish trust.

Folding board

A group of four goes together on a mat. One child lies on his back on the mat, arms by the side of the body. One spotter stands by the head and reaches at first underneath the head, then under the shoulders. The other two spotters stand right next to the shoulders and reach around the upper

arms, close to the armpit (Fig. 51). One has to wait until the lying person is stiff like a board in order to lift him to a stand. The "board" is put down again very slowly, using the same spotting technique (Fig. 52).

Floater

A group of eight assembles on a mat. One child lies down on his back, arms to his side. One spotter stands by the head and reaches at first under the head, then the shoulders. Two other spotters stand right next to the shoulders and reach around the upper arms close to the armpit. The next two (strongest) children stand at the height of the hips and reach underneath the seat. The last two spotters stand at the knee and reach under the upper and lower leg. The spotters have to wait until the child lying down is stiff like a board in order to lift his hips high into the horizontal. Slowly and carefully the floater is brought back to the floor (Fig. 56.1-56.2).

Fig. 56.1-56.2: Floater

Hint:

Because the legs are lighter they are usually lifted too fast and the floater finds himself in a bent position. Adaptation of all spotters is required.

Variations:

• The group walks with the floater forward, backward, sideways or turns him.

• The group carries the floater overhead (grip change underneath the body and go close underneath)

• The group puts the floater onto his feet.

• The group places the floater onto a bench or box.

Communication and Cooperation

Like all social manners of behavior, the ability to cooperate is important. One must learn to engage with and submit to a partner. Verbal, as well as non-verbal agreements must take place, in order to provide solutions for problems. Within the field of spotting and securing, there are also movement problems that are approached with the goals in mind, to succeed to a situation and to successfully achieve a solution within the small group of the spotter team. To further the ability to cooperate means to further the ability of the team.

The following game types are meant to further team work and problem solving behaviors between partners and in groups. The children must find the tasks worthwhile and enticing in order for them to be appealing. For such tasks, one should start with groups of two and then increase to three or more.

For the following group formations the atom game (see above) helps to form accidental groups in the desired size.

Big number/form creation

Following a run the children find each other in groups of two, three or larger – depending on the task. They now try to illustrate together, with their body (standing or lying) those numbers. Agreements must be made.

Variations:

• Upon call of higher numbers, geometrical forms should be illustrated, for example triangles, squares, ellipses.

• Given forms should be created with eyes closed.

Open, liberal tasks

Through agreements, common movements should be found:

• "Two of you pick a synchronized movement sequence. Combine for example running, hopping forward and backward, squat down and straight jump."

• "What could you do as a pair or in threes where all of you must somehow touch each other?" (Fig. 57)

• In fours: "Find a solution for one of you to be carried."

Fig. 57: Creative moves as pair, in touch with each other

Statue/Monument

The children are running criss-cross through the gym. Upon the call "two", two children find each other spontaneously and create a statue. The frozen picture/monument is judged, commentated upon and possibly corrected by the game leader, and at last dissolves, upon the call of a pass word. The children continue to run and "mix" again. Now "three" might be called ... (Fig. 58).

Fig. 58: Statue

Fig. 59: Picture on the wall

Picture on the wall

The children stand as a group of people, like in an artistic picture, tightly together and pretend to be frozen. Upon the call "midnight" or "ghost hour", they start to move very slowly to the right and left without detaching from the wall Upon call "one o'clock" the ghost hour is over and the children need to stand again as a picture (Fig. 59).

Group picture

Five to seven group members form a group sculpture. One child is the tourist who takes pictures. When the children think they are ready with their sculpture they yell out loud: "Picture!" After the picture has been taken they collapse together in slow motion. (Fig. 60). The photographer may decide which sculpture he liked the best.

Fig. 60: Group picture

Flower lawn

Four children sit or stand in a circle and hold hands. Upon the call "sun", the single groups blossom as flowers. Upon the call "night", the flower closes. The groups should try the creation of the flower before the teacher calls it.

Fig. 61: Car drive

Car drive

A group of five illustrates a car with a driver; four children are the wheels and roll simultaneously forward or backward and around corners. The wheels can be shown as forward or backward rolls or as cartwheels. The driver imitates the steering (Fig. 61).

At the hair dresser

Six or more children stand close together and lift their arms. They all form a head, the arms are the hair. One of the children is the hair dresser and pretends that he is combing the hair with a gigantic comb and is blow drying it. If he blow-dries it in pantomime fashion from the bottom, the hair spikes up, like in punk style. The hair dresser can also separate the hair in the middle, or curl it. Due to a lot of blow-drying the arms can also show split hair with the hands as finale.

Newspaper run

Cooperation through mutual understanding: Two children grasp a double paged newspaper at its corners and run from one side of the gym to the other. At that point the newspaper is folded in half and grasped at all four corners, and the two run back. "Which pair has the smallest newspaper in the end?" Assuming all papers are the same size, the winner is the pair that finishes first. If the paper tears one must run one more time (depending on prior agreement, from the beginning, or just the last leg), the other paper half would then be the (new) substitute.

"Chinese ball throwing- and ball catching machine"

Two hold a larger towel, sheet or board etc. by the corners (=ball throwing or catching machine). At first a ball is balanced on top of this, then it's thrown up in the air and is caught again (Fig. 62).

Variations:

Fig. 62: Throwing and catching machine

*   The ball is thrown with the towel against the wall, and must be caught again.

*   One or two children throw a ball from outside onto the ball catching machine. Depending on the condition of the surface or type of ball, it is thrown right back.

"Catch-throw-surfaces": pillow covers, towels, large double page newspaper (possibly three papers glued together and reinforced at the corners with tape).

Balls: balloons, soft balls of different sizes, ping pong balls and tennis balls, Japanese balls made out of paper and beach balls.

Equipment rally

Setting up and taking down equipment not only teaches familiarity with it, but also tests common social actions and experience. In preparation for the action, certain game types with large and small pieces of equipment are

appropriate, and allow them to experience social interaction. Small gymnastics type equipment like mats, small boxes or parts of them (depending on size of the equipment and age of the children) can be transported over short distances in groups of four or six. Simultaneously, the cooperation during set-up change, and putting the equipment back becomes a habit.

Hint:
In order to avoid a hectic situation and the danger of getting injured, additional rules need to be made. For example, if carrying hands cannot hold on, because of too much speed, the group starts again from the beginning. Quality before quantity!

Cooperative Catching Games

For children at elementary age, tag games are very popular, because they fulfill their desire for movement. In context with spotting and securing, the following examples of tag games mention only those that contain cooperative characteristics. Thus, the freeing of a caught partner is always an essential part. The ego-oriented child learns to temporarily waive his own attitude on behalf of common interests. To step in for somebody, or to save somebody, can become a gripping game. A longer "time out," due to being caught is consequently not very satisfactory.

Triangle catch

Three children hold hands and form a triangle. A fourth child stands outside and can only then become a triangle member or be exchanged, when he has tagged off one child of the triangle. The two other triangle children try to protect the third one in such ways that they position themselves so cleverly that the catcher has a hard time to get to him. Body contact with the exception of tagging off is not allowed.

Catching and freeing

One child is the tagger, or the teacher also tries to tag off the children. The ones who are tagged off sit down on the floor. He can be freed when another child touches one while running by and calls "free". Should the tagger manage to tag everyone, he becomes the king of the taggers. If the game lasts too long, the game leader steps in and designates a new tagger.

Variations:

- The tagged off child remains standing in straddle stance and can be freed by crawling underneath.

- Two taggers can be used for larger groups.

Magic

A child tries to tag other children with a colorful carton stick (inside roll of paper towels) and cast a spell on them. Those tagged

- remain standing as if they are frozen

- turn into animals

- fall to the floor

The remaining free children try to free the ones under the spell through briefly copying their body posture in front of them.

Learn to Listen

For communication as part of cooperation, and therefore also for the spotting of children amongst themselves, it is important that children lend each other their attention and acknowledgment, so that everyone dares to speak up. Especially shy children profit from this, when they, for once, find themselves in the center of attention, or when they are allowed to demonstrate. It provides them with the opportunity to do something in front of a group without failing right away. They have an opportunity to succeed.

Game suggestion: "Now it's you!"

The children sit in smaller circles together. The first child performs for example a gymnastics skill, the others copy it. Hereafter he points to the next child (or neighbor) and says: "Now it's your turn!" Thus he is freed and the next one demonstrates something new.

1.2   Reaction Games and Games to Awaken Alertness

The awakening of alertness, and the challenging of concentration and reaction abilities create the basis for what follows in the gymnastics lesson with regard to qualified spotting, securing and accompanying. At the beginning of the lesson, tasks should be posed for spotter activities that demand such abilities from the children. The following game types contain, additionally to the other types, an improvement of alertness for the following gymnastics tasks, if they are developed through criss-cross running with calls and fast reaction. Thus, the free criss-cross running through the gym is again, for the following games, the initial starting point.

During the run the teacher calls out a signal word:

Change
Upon call take different positions (if need be, through prior agreements): Prone position, lying on back, lying on side, candle stick, sit, squat, relevé . . .

Freeze
Upon a signal word remain stiff or frozen: "Who is still wobbling?" (Check body tension).

Hint:
Only a tight body can be carried and guided satisfactorily during spotting. This game type with a tight body prepares the children well for the following gymnastics tasks, where body tension is required, for example: handstand, partner acrobatics . . .

"Simon says, hop!"
The children run freely in the gym. At first, the teacher (later a child) is at the long side of the gym and calls to the children to hop, run, walk, jump, laugh, crawl, wave. But they are only allowed to do it if they call Simon says beforehand: "Simon says, . . ." If only the activity is called all remain standing. Example: "Simon says, jump!", and all children jump through the gym, if the call is "run", all children remain standing, because "Simon says" wasn't added to the call. "The one who runs despite of it? . . . was asleep!"

Hint:

In between one should call "Simon says, run!" in order to assure a movement-intense game.

Day and Night

The children sit in pairs, facing each other at the gym middle line. The children on one side are the day, the others are the night. Upon the teacher's call "Day", the named ones run away, those sitting opposite need to try to catch the runner. The caught ones must go to the other side.

Hints:

- The children should not run all the way to the wall in order to avoid injuries, but when running over a certain designated line in front of the wall they are freed from getting caught.
- For children it's always nicer and more gripping to work the signal word into a story.

Fire-Water-Earth

This game is known by a lot of children. It belongs to the most popular reaction games amongst elementary school children. For this game a prior agreed upon action follows the call of a signal word (Fig. 63).

Fig. 63: "Water!"

Hints:

- In gymnastics it is advantageous to include the already set up equipment.

- For smaller children it is advisable to include the signal words (no more than three) in a story. Once these words occur in the story they immediately have to react.

- The game receives the character of unity when part of the children are named firemen, and in case of catastrophes they need to grab civilians in order to save them.

The signal words can be:
"Fire!":

- All children must walk fast to the emergency exit (reality related).

- Or run into a corner of the gym.

- Or the firemen must quickly grab a civilian in order to save him.

"Water!":

- All children run onto elevations (boxes, bars, benches...), in order to save themselves from high water. And the firemen can be in action again (Fig. 63).

"Earth!":
- All lie down flat on the floor (because, for example, the emergency helicopter is landing).

Additions and/ or variations:

"Lightning!":
- The children look quickly for a lightning deflector (for example rubber mats).

"Storm!":
- The children look for protection underneath the apparatus.

"Sun!":
- Warning is over, the children can turn around and sunbathe.

Driving a car

1st gear (walk), 2nd gear (slow run), 3rd gear (run), 4th gear (sprint), reverse gear.

Hint:

With the inclusion of a partner the "initiation of contact" can additionally be fostered (see above).

Catching fish

The gym is the wide ocean or a lake. In the corners is the home of different types of fish: According to agreements there is a tuna fish corner, a crab fish corner, a shrimp corner and a cat fish corner (when it's a lake choose lake fish). A quarter of the entire group is in each corner. One child (or the teacher) is in the middle of the gym as a fisherman and calls at the beginning of the game: "I call all tuna fish!" ... one after another to him into the sea, until all are "swimming" in it. Now the fisherman calls: "The sea is quiet!" and all fish remain in their location. Then he calls: "The sea is stormy!" and all fish jump and hop in the sea. This is repeated a few times until he calls:

Fig. 64: Catching fish: "Stormy sea!"

"Ebb!" All children must now quickly run back into their corners because the fisherman is now allowed to catch fish. The one who gets tagged off becomes a fisherman helper until the sea is empty (Fig. 64).

The shark comes!
Set out a newspaper which represents an island for each child present. The children run freely through the gym without touching the newspapers. Upon the call "the shark is coming", the children have to move quickly to an "island". In the further course of the game the smaller islands unfortunately "sink", which means the newspapers are removed so that more children have to fit onto fewer newspapers. The game is stopped when it cannot continue further without repeating.

Variation:
- He who doesn't find a place becomes the shark who swims in the outer parts and scares the children upon the call "here comes the shark".

Atom game
The children run freely in the gym. Upon call of a number they find each other quickly together in that number (Fig. 65). At "one", they remain standing. The numbers keep changing.

Variations:
- Whoever remains left alone receives minus points.

- Or he could perform a special task (for example 10 hops on one leg, a push-up, a candle stick, a head stand, a cartwheel or a handstand).

Fig. 65: Atom game: "Go! 3!"

Hints:
If a certain number is necessary for the following gymnastics session at stations, it's advisable to call that particular number of group members during the last run-through. This not only helps to forming a quick organization, but it also leads to random group formations.

Atom game with hand holding

The children run freely in the gym. Upon call of a certain number they find themselves together in that number. The children now reach quickly for their hands and simultaneously form a circle, and then, as a sign of "completeness", raise their arms.

Hints:

- Through this game the opportunity for touch contact is increased.
- The teacher should animate the children to wide room patterns, and avoid calling the numbers too rapidly one after another, in order to bring about new personal formations of the "atoms".

Variations:

- Upon "three" run in threes, while only five legs are allowed to touch the floor.
- Upon "four" continue in fours, while two arms and six legs may touch the floor, etc.

Shadow run

One child runs in front and demonstrates body movements and directions. One to two children try to quickly copy the demonstrator.

Hint:

This task teaches the ability to adapt to a partner.

1.3   Partner and Group Acrobatics

Partner and group acrobatics are ideal for experiencing cooperation, the putting of trust into someone, responsibility, and care. In order to achieve the artistic trick, all social forms become necessary here.

Prerequisites, like support strength and total body tension, are at a minimum. Even though acrobatics teaches this, special exercise forms should be continuously offered for preparation and should be parallel to all others.

All the following figures and small pyramids are listed systematically, building upon each other. The sequence suggests indirectly a methodical approach. Only figures were chosen that are suitable for school and gym clubs.

Fundamentals

Health
- The children must know what **body tension** is.
  Only when all muscles are tightened strongly, can the desired joint positions be maintained. Then a child is stable for loads and forces aimed at the joints. Thus, an arched back means a lack of tension in the stomach and seat muscles.
- The children must know how **to straighten the back** for the carrying bench position by pulling in the stomach. They cannot operate with a back that "hangs through".
- One should never step onto the unstable spinal column or the kidney area, only **onto the pelvis area (seat) or the shoulder girdle area**. Children forget to pay attention to this during learning and practicing. The teacher must constantly remind them.

Occupation of the positions
Children in small groups should match in weight. For homogenous groups each child should at least try the positions once above and below. Often the bottom position is not well liked with children, each child prefers to stand, kneel or lie on top. *Exceptions* are pre-school children who shouldn't be the bottom person when practicing with school

children. Furthermore, the teacher regulates the role divisions *when it's not possible* to place *all* children on the bottom or top due to different body sizes and weights. Finally, the stronger and more stable child is the bottom person when it comes to experimenting and demonstrating.

Build-up and down
- Partners may only be mounted very carefully with the utmost caution, without hurting the carrying child.
- The mounting and climbing up should happen slowly and be concentrated, not abruptly. Afterward one cannot just simply jump down. The children need to climb down and if necessary reach hands. Landing smoothly must also be learned. Jumping off must be practiced. There are special techniques for this.

Dress code
- Children should be barefooted or wear gymnastics shoes.
- No jewelry, of course.
- The children should wear tightly fitting clothes. Slick, shiny warm-up suits are not suitable.

Floor
- Practice should take place on mats or padded areas. Small boxes can be included as sitting or standing areas for the formation of the pyramid, or as part of it.

Technical hints
- For bench positions, *arms and thighs* should form *a 90-degree angle* with the floor. Arms are straight (be aware of hyper-extended arms with girls).
- *Legs* are *slightly separated* and arms are placed shoulder-width apart.
- The figures *must be explained thoroughly*. Drawings (enlarged) are helpful.
- One to two children should *be ready for spotting* in order to offer helping hands that help secure balance (see also the following chapter "Simple spotting", chapter B I. 2, p. 131ff.).
- The children should be encouraged to come to *mutual agreements*.

Basic "Bench" Position

The basic "bench" position is characterized through (see Fig. 66):
- Support on shins and knees in knee stand and support of the hands.
- Arms are supported shoulder-width apart, exactly underneath the shoulder girdle in a 90-degree angle with the floor or to the trunk. Hands are placed flat on the floor and point forward (Fig. 66a).
- Legs are slightly separated and knees are below the seat, which means the knee as well as the leg-trunk-angle form a 90-degree angle. Thus, the thigh is right-angled to the floor (Fig. 66b).
- The back must be kept straight and may not hang through. Therefore, the stomach muscles must be tightened ("pull in stomach"). The head should be kept in extension with the trunk (head in neck = arched back!). It's helpful to look at the floor(Fig. 66c).

After introducing the correct execution for the bench position (partner control and correction from outside) the children may try different small figures. At first the base positions of the upper person can be tried on a real bench or box, instead of on the "human" bench.

Fig. 66: A perfect basic "bench" position

This is only recommended as support for the knees and hands. A fully embracing methodical introduction, which also includes preparatory exercises and apparatus aids, is waived, because *unity is the focal point of this chapter.* Spotter activities that secure balance belong to the training process of acrobats. Hints are given in the following exercises.

Water bed

Two to four children go next to each other into a bench position, another child lies in prone position on top of the created water bed. The bed begins to sway (Fig. 67a).

Fig. 67a-f: Acrobatic figures base on "benches"

Scale
One child forms a bench, a second one lies with good body tension in a prone position on top (Fig. 67b).

Variations:
- Change direction to the lower bench (parallel and across).
- Try lying on back in various directions.

Bench constructions
One child goes into the bench position, another one puts his feet, lower leg or thigh (depending on the ability) on top of the bench and supports with straight arms into a push-up position (Fig. 67c).

Variations:
- Parallel or from different sides.
- Reverse or frontal push-up.

- The bench person and/or push-up person lifts one leg straight up (Fig. 67d).

Mirror picture

One child goes into the bench position, another lies on top, exactly back to back, reaches with his arms around the trunk of the bottom person and lifts the legs to vertical.

Variation:

- Direction of the upper person (Fig. 67e/f).

Double Bench Pyramids and More

Double bench

One partner goes into the bench position on a mat. Hands are positioned shoulder-width apart, legs are slightly separated. Arms and thighs are in a right angle to the trunk, back is tightened and straight (no arch!). The second partner now tries to kneel in bench position on top, supporting on the pelvis or shoulder girdle (not the spine), first in the same direction as the bottom person, then in counter direction (Fig. 68a/b).

Hint:

In order to climb on top, an elevated climbing aid, for example a box, can be placed parallel to the kneeling child.

Variation:

- One leg of the upper person can be straightened forward backwards, possibly also lift opposite arm (Fig. 68c).

Heavy double bench

The bottom person goes into bench position, the upper one sits down onto the tightened, straight back of the lower person, hands placed on seat and feet on shoulder girdle (or as variation, reversed). Then the upper person pushes up to a reverse bench (Fig. 68e/f).

Note:

The reverse bench can also be used in the lower position, but is generally difficult to arrange in amateur gymnastics.

Fig. 68a-i: Double "benches" pyramids

Triple benches

- Two children form a bench next to each other, a third child forms a bench on top of the two, looking in the same direction (Fig. 68d).
- Two children go feet to feet into bench position, a third child creates a bench parallel on top of the pelvis area (Fig. 68h).
- Two children go head to head into the bench position, at short distance, a third one creates a bench parallel on top of the shoulders (Fig. 68g).

Variation:

- The upper bench person can straighten the back leg from a knee support and possibly lift the opposite arm into the horizontal (Fig. 68c).

Town musicians from Bremen (a famous statue of animals in Germany)

A third child the "rooster" mounts on top of a double benches (the donkey and the cat) with climbing aid or spotter (Fig. 68i).

High wheel barrel

Three children go together. One child goes into bench position, the second child goes into push-up position with straight arms, feet on the floor, hands on top of the seat of the partner. The third child lifts the feet of the second child to a high push-up position with the knees slightly bent (Fig. 69a).

Hint:

The children are allowed to bend a little bit at the hips in a push-up position in order to avoid an arch.

Nevertheless, should they not be able to keep good body extension, they should straddle their legs, and the carrying child goes in between the legs in order to lift at the knees or thighs.

Variation:

• The upper position supports on top of the shoulders above the bench position and puts his feet on top of the shoulder of a standing child who is to the rear bench (Fig. 69b).

a  b

Fig. 69a/b: High wheel barrel

Bench Positions with Kneeling Upper Person

High knee stand

One child goes into bench position. One child kneels down to a heel sit (feet toward the head) on top of the seat area (it's advisable to support on a small box that is placed in front of the feet of the bench position). Once balance is established, the upper person rises to high knee stand (Fig. 70a).

Fig. 70a-d: Benches with kneeling and standing upper person

One legged-high knee stand

One child goes into bench position. Another child positions himself into a heel sit over the bench position (with support of both hands on the shoulders of the bottom person), and puts one foot down for a one-legged knee stand (Fig. 70b).

Bench Positions with Standing Upper Person

Hint:

For mounting on top of a bottom person in bench position it is advisable to always start the first attempts from a box, then with the helping hand of a child.

High stand "with banister"

One child goes into bench position, a second one stands straddling the bottom person and supports himself on top of the shoulders. A third child now climbs onto the seat of the bench positioned child, supporting himself with the arms on the standing child's shoulder (Fig. 70c).

Variation:

- The standing child is in front of the bench and supports himself on the shoulders, or behind the bench on the seat. The third child, standing on top of the bench, stands on the opposite support surface (shoulder or pelvis area) (Fig. 70d).

High straddle stand

One child goes into bench position. A second child mounts from the side with his whole foot on top of the seat, then with the other foot on the shoulder girdle, rises up and spreads the arms to the side, or holds hands on the hips (Fig. 71).

Fig. 71: High straddle stand

High lunge

One child is in bench position. A second child mounts with the whole foot sideways to the bench position, on top of the seat, then onto the shoulder girdle, rises up while bending the front leg and spreads the arms to the side or upwards (Fig. 72).

Fig. 72: High lunge

Viewing position

One child goes into bench position. A second child mounts with both feet sideways to the bench position on top of the seat, rises up and puts one hand against the forehead in order to "look far" (Fig. 73).

Variation:

- Change of direction (Fig. 74).

or

Fig. 73   *Fig. 74*

Flamingo on a stone

One child goes into bench position. A second child mounts sideways on top of the bench with both feet on top of the seat, rises up and tries (with balancing aid) to lift one leg (Fig. 75). Hint: Arms are in side position.

Fig. 76: Small scale

Variation:
- Small scale (Fig. 76).

Fig. 75: Flamingo

Straddle stand on top of two benches

- Two children get close to each other in bench position, a third child performs a straddle stand on both seats of the bottom children, looking in the same direction (Fig. 77).

- Two children go feet against feet in bench position, a third child goes into straddle stand on top of both seats of the bottom children and spreads arms to the side (Fig. 78).

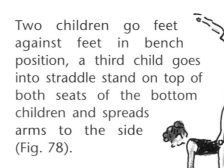

Fig. 77: On two benches

Fig. 78: On top of two seats

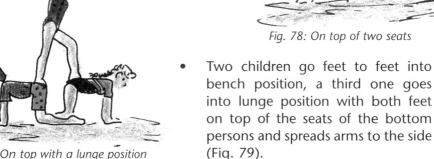

- Two children go feet to feet into bench position, a third one goes into lunge position with both feet on top of the seats of the bottom persons and spreads arms to the side (Fig. 79).

Fig. 79: On top with a lunge position

Foursome-bench-stand-pyramids

All above mentioned double pyramids, where the bottom person is in bench position and the upper one is standing on both or one leg, in frontal or side position, can be doubled next to each other by holding hands with the upper children, and can be connected to a pyramid (Fig. 80).

Fig. 80: Benches pyramid for four

Push-up Acrobatics

The push-up chain

One child goes into push-up position, arms are straight and placed shoulder width apart. A second child goes in front of the first child into push-up position and puts his feet on the shoulders of the first child in order to achieve a higher position. More children can build in front in the same way (Fig. 81a).

Twisted, double push-ups

One child goes into a frontal or reverse push-up position. The second child supports himself by reaching for the ankles, and puts his feet onto the shoulders of the partner into push-up position (Fig. 81b).

Hint:

The reverse push-up is somewhat difficult and only works with strong children. Therefore, these task variations are best suited for selected students.

Fig. 81a/b

121

Bottom Lying Position

Double Decker (biplane)

One child is in lying on his back, another child goes in opposite direction with straddled legs on top of the partner in push-up position. He reaches one foot to the lying child and raises to a tight, extended push-up position, while the bottom child keeps holding on to both ankles (Fig. 82).

Fig. 82: Double decker

Air push-up

One child lies on his back on the floor with bent knees, arms reaching toward the ceiling. The other child supports himself, moving on the knees, above the bottom person to a push-up position. With a light push off the floor the lying child pushes at the knees of the partner "into the air" to an "air push-up" (Fig. 83), ... something for the advanced.

Fig. 83: Air push-up

L-sit

A child lies with legs tucked on the floor, arms are stretched toward the ceiling. The other child sits on the knees and holds on to them, then lifts one leg, then the second to a long sit with supportive grip of the bottom child (Fig. 84).

Fig. 84: L-sit

Small and big flying people

For flying people, it's a prerequisite to have good body tension in order to succeed. One child is lying on his back, arms and legs up in a right angle to the trunk. The second child stands in front of the legs and puts his hands into the those of the partner. For the "small flyer" the child lies on top of the lower tucked legs of the bottom child and is lifted to horizontal (very suitable for small children) (Fig. 85.1-85.3).

Fig. 85.1-85.3: Small flying people

Fig. 86: Big flying people

For the "big flyer" the bottom child places his feet with bent legs under the hips of the top child (toes point to the outside). The supporting legs straighten into vertical. The center of gravity of the "flyer" must now lie exactly above the feet of the lying person. Those who are good at this may spread their arms to the side. A third child can assist in keeping balance; many can try this trick (Fig. 86).

Variation:
• Balancing aid is given by the feet.

Fallbackers ... a test of courage

The action is similar to the flyer, only that the courageous child sits on the feet of the bottom child. With two side positioned spotters that help with the back, the upper child now lies very tight with the shoulders back into the hands of the lying child, and lifts the legs to straighten the body. (Fig. 87.1-87.2).

Fig. 87.1-87.2: Fallbackers

Shoulder stand

One child is lying on his back with tucked legs, arms stretched upward. A second child stands in straddle stand, right and left at the height of the knees and supports himself with straight arms on the knees. Then he moves forward with his shoulders into the hands of the lying child, at the same time one leg swings backward and upward. The

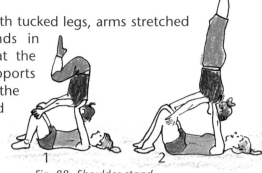

Fig. 88: Shoulder stand

second leg follows quickly to a shoulder stand. Two children at the sides can reach for the thighs and guide into the shoulder stand (also see the spotter grip for handstands, p. 169) (Fig. 129).

Hint:

A professional way to go into the shoulder stand is, as in a headstand (Fig. 89.1-89.4), to first tuck in the legs in order to bring the seat over the shoulders and then to stretch the legs into the vertical position.

Fig. 89.1-89.4: Headstand

Climber onto the "Chair"

Frontal climb up

When a child climbs up onto a supporting child, the supporter should always initally have a resistive force to act against, meaning a sturdy resistance underneath the body; for example a small box, a bench for elementary school children, or another child in bench position (Fig. 90A-C). With increasing capabilities, the supporting child can also lean against a wall before beginning the poses (Fig. 90D). The mounting child should start from an elevation, so that the center of gravity is already almost at the desired height. With completion of the pose the two children reach around their lower arms, that means the extended body should be leaning back. The hands can slide into a handhold (Fig. 90a). At first the upper child should step with one foot onto the knee, erect the upper body, and then place the

second leg. As the body leans back, and the legs are slightly extended, the supporting child starts to rise as well. A spotting child can support the back (Fig. 90E). Skilled children can release one hand. For advanced children, the "chair" can also change grips and hold the legs (Fig. 90b). When a third child plays the carrying bench, he can now slide into the prone position.

Fig. 90A-E and 90a/b

Rearward climb-up

The conditions for a rearward climb-up are similar to those for the previous description. The supporting child reaches around the hips when the first foot is planted. In a rearward stand one can hold further down the legs in order to attain a more forward lean.

Tip:

Another child can also counter-support at the stomach in order to prevent a falling forward. During demonstrations a pose can be struck similar to the previous exercises (for example lunge step with one arm to the side).

Mounting onto the Thighs: Galleons Figure

Two bottom children stand foot to foot next to each other with slightly bent knees in straddle stand. A third child supports himself on top of the shoulders of the partner and mounts from behind onto the thigh, placing the foot close to the hip bend, while pulling up gently by the shoulders. The bottom person clamps the thigh with his arms. The top person now releases the hands from the shoulders and spreads them to the side (see photo, p. 129). This can be continued as a chain with adding two more children (Fig. 91).

Hint:

Mounting from an elevation facilitates quick success.

Fig. 91: Galleons figure

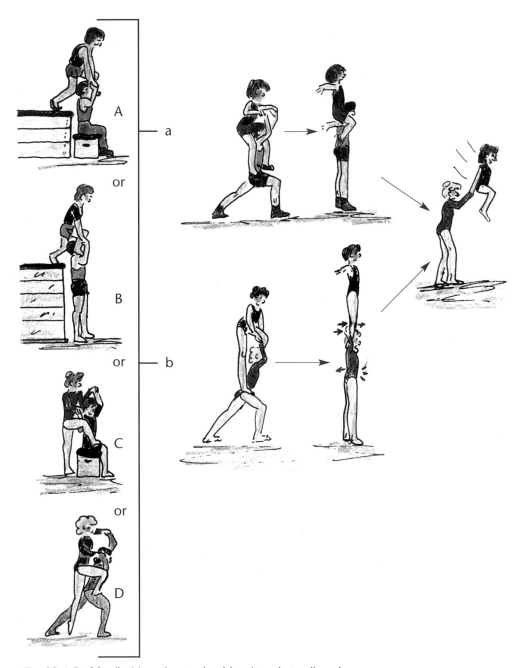

Fig. 92 A-D, 92 a/b: Mounting to shoulder sit and standing above

Mounting to Shoulder Sit
and Standing on Top of Each Other

Shoulder sit

In order to sit on top of a partner's shoulders the mounting child starts from behind the carrier and grasps for the highly held hands. Initially the supporting children should sit on a small box. This facilitates the balancing of the body under the load of mounting, and on the shoulders sitting of the child. Furthermore, it prevents the back from arching under the load. The mounting child also mounts from an elevation onto the shoulders in order to position the center of gravity almost at seat height. In further attempts one can climb onto the standing child from a high box, and later can practice mounting onto the thigh. Finally, in the fourth learning step, the child mounts from the floor onto the straddled partners, standing with knees slightly bent (Fig. 92a).

The crowning: Standing on top of each other!

The mounting child can also climb to a standing position on top of the shoulders. The methodical approach with equipment aids is similar to the shoulder sit (see above and Fig. 92 A-C). As the hands are released and the standing child straightens, the supporting child reaches around the calves of the standing child (Fig. 92b).

Fig. 93 Combinations of different acrobatic figures

Combinations of Acrobatic Poses

Finally, the many possibilities for basic pose combinations for groups of children should be pointed out. Stand or knee scales, headstands and held handstands round off the picture of a successful group formation. That does not always mean that the formations have to be symmetrical. More exciting are often the simple, but in themselves, different poses (Fig. 93, p. 128).

For further, especially more sophisticated ideas, one should consult the literature hints at the end of the book.

2 Second Level: Simple Spotting

The teacher or coach should *use every chance* to let the children experience spotting assistance in simple and controlled situations. The teacher must check every gymnastics situation to decide if spotting can be included. Children can, for example, lift themselves onto the apparatus and secure landings while reaching around the stomach and back area. Teachers should constantly encourage such spotting actions. With such tasks children grow naturally into more complex spotting actions, and spotting becomes a second nature.

A start into spotting on all apparatus can happen through easy spotter activities. Those are, from a point of view of spotter-grip-onset, uncomplicated. The choice of location is, at first, of lesser importance and an incorrect spotter behavior is not yet dangerous. The following presents a few examples:

Balance Apparatus

Balancing aid

Three children position themselves next to the apparatus that they are going to balance on (for example a rounded beam, reversed bench, low beam, rope). The children reach for each other's hands, as in a chain in sideward position to the balancing apparatus. The middle child balances over the apparatus and attempts small leaps and jumps. The other two walk along on the sides, securing the balancing gymnast.

Variation:

The children practice in pairs, one child reaches his hands to the other and assists his balancing act. When the gymnast performs a turn they change hands.

Fig. 94: Securing

Securing while balancing

- One spotter holds the helping hand at trunk height of the balancing gymnast, who can reach for it if necessary (Fig. 94, p. 131).
- One or two spotters secure by keeping their hands ready around the stomach and back.

Securing landings during jump downs

The practicing gymnast performs a straight jump off the beam or a box. One to two children try to "grasp" the gymnast before the landing. Through "forking" with the close hand at the back and the far one on the stomach, they prevent the gymnast from falling forward or backward (Fig. 120, p. 162).

Hang and Support Apparatus

Grip securing at the wrist

- One child hangs on the rings, rope, or bars in tuck hang. Two children reach with both hands around each wrist of the hanging person and secure him from slipping off.
- One child performs a turn over forward or backward in a tucked position, two children secure the wrists (Fig. 178a/b, p. 201).

Front support and jump to front support

The simplest spot is to offer the folded hands as a heightened push-off surface (similar to when one mounts a horse) for mounting into support.

When jumping up to support the following spot is advisable: Two children stand at jump-off height and reach around the thighs of the gymnast. The gymnast bounces twice on the spot and then jumps into front support. The lifting children assist with support grip at the thigh (possibly also at the center of gravity) to transport the body to support (at the bar). Also, in order to experience a fully elevated front support, the spotting children can assist the child in front support by pushing up at the thighs.

Chin-ups on high bar

The children reach with both hands around one thigh of the hanging gymnast at a time. With every chin-up the child is supported in his upward motion, due to the help from underneath the center of gravity (Fig. 179, p. 201).

Rotational, push-off, or lift assistance for turning in and over backward, or hanging from one or two knees on high bar, uneven bars, parallel bars, rings and ropes

The gymnast goes into a squat-hang-stand and extends one foot to another child. The spotter leads the foot overhead. Because of the elevated push-off location of the lifted leg, the center of gravity can, through bending of the leg, be lifted so high that it reaches over the head. Many children go with the free foot to the bar (or similar, the grip location) and push themselves, because of its resistance, into the backward rotation for a further push-off.

For very weak children the first lifted leg is being led by the spotters directly to the bar in order to stem with the bottom of the foot against the bar, so he can hold on. By moving the second leg close and tucking up the legs, they can also lift the center of gravity (seat) over head (Fig. 184, p. 204).

Securing of the knee bend in knee hang or during swing off

At first two children, then only one, secure the holding of the deep knee bend while gently pushing down with both hands onto the lower legs/feet. When swinging off the spotters have to adapt to up and downward movements of the lower legs in order to avoid too much pressure on the back side of the knees (Fig. 95)

Fig. 95: Knee hang

Securing landings when dismounting and jumping down

The practicing gymnast jumps or performs a dismount off an apparatus. One to two children attempt to catch the body of the gymnast before the landing while "forking" him in with the close hand on the back and the far hand on the stomach, in order to prevent a falling forward or backward (Fig. 96).

Examples:
- Cast from support off the bar to a stand.
- Under-swing on the bars or rings.
- Jump off from sitting on a bar.

Climbing aids at the ropes

One child jumps into a tucked, bent arm hang onto a rope. One partner stands by the rope and secures it, reaching shortly below the feet. The hanging child can now stand on the spotters' hands and push up with the help of the legs. The procedure is repeated with every new pull (Fig. 180, p. 201).

Vaulting Apparatus

Climbing aid onto apparatus

When "discovering movement possibilities," and for obstacle gymnastics over higher boxes, small children can give themselves a climbing aid when mounting. Just like with the "rider's aid," the helping child folds the hands in such a way that another one can stand on them. With support onto the apparatus, the climbing child can now push off the helping hands in order to get onto the apparatus with the swinging leg.

Fig. 96: Securing the landing

Securing the landing

The practicing gymnast jumps off a box or vault. One to two children attempt to catch the gymnast's body before the landing, and through forking in with the one hand on the front, and the other hand on the back, prevent a fall forward or backward (Fig. 96).

Hint:

Same spot as with dismounts and jump downs from apparatus.

Floor and Gymnastics Skills

Straight jump with partner assistance

Support grip on upper arm. Two spotters stand in front of the gymnast and reach around the upper arm. The inner hand reaches for the armpit and the outer one clamps around the upper arm. The gymnast bounces twice on the floor and then jumps, with the lifting support of the two spotters, up in the

air. The lifting spotters must stand close to the gymnast and lift energetically upon take-off (Fig. 107, 108, p. 150).

Support of continuous gymnastics jumps

Three children stand next to each other, the middle one is the jumper. The inner hand reaches from behind under the armpit of the gymnast. The middle child places his hand onto the outer hand in order to be able to support himself upward later on. At first the children run through the gym using this spotter grip, so they learn to adapt to a mutual rhythm. Thereupon the running continues with cat, scissors and split leaps, with the spotters assisting the upward motion each time (Fig. 124a-e, p. 167).

The teacher should, as a rhythmic aid, accompany the movement verbally: "Run, run, cat leap, run . . ." or "Run, run scissors leap . . ." Later on the children should accompany each other.

Support exercises (wheel barrel)

One child goes with slightly straddled legs into push-up position. One spotter goes between the legs, reaches from outside around the thighs and lifts the legs off the floor. Supporting himself, the gymnast moves forward (Fig. 97).

Fig. 97: Wheel barrel

Aid for tension exercises out of a back lying position and for the frontal and reverse push-up

One spotter stands halfway squatting down in front of the practicing person, reaches for the feet and lifts the gymnast with tightened seat and stomach muscles (Fig. 98).

Stand up aid for the forward roll

Fig. 98: Reverse push-up

- One child stands facing the gymnast approximately two feet in front of his standing location. He reaches his hands toward the gymnast to "catch" him and pulls him up.

- Two children are standing opposite each other at the standing position (in a right angle to the rolling person) and stretch the far hand toward the gymnast. The close hand goes under the upper arm and supports while raising the upper body (Fig. 99).

Fig. 99: Spotter grip for raising the body

Aid for the introduction of rolling movements

Two children stand shoulder to shoulder, a third child squats exactly in front of them supporting himself on his hands. The spotters only offer their inner hand to hold in the gymnast's feet (tucked position is maintained). The spotters hold the feet while the practicing person extends the legs. The spotters may push a little in the direction of the movement (Fig. 126, p. 168).

Handstand with apparatus aid

The gymnast performs a handstand from a box or in front of a wall. Two children stand close to the hands, reach around the thigh and bring the gymnast into the vertical and then back toward the apparatus (Fig. 102, p. 143).

Partner and Group Acrobatics

Hand reaching or grasping of the hips from behind as balancing aid when climbing up onto the bottom person

For figures where a child mounts onto a "bench" that has been formed by another child, a partner should be ready to offer a hand to assist with balancing and serve as a possible support base (Fig. 100a/b). It's also advantageous to reach around the hips from behind. Better stability can be achieved with two spotters that support under the armpit with one hand and hold the hand with the other.

Balancing aid for completed poses

In general balancing aid can also be given, as is described above, for complete poses.

For poses in which a child tries to keep balance, one can assist at hands and feet (Fig. 100c) or other suitable body parts (Fig. 100d). For certain poses one can counter-support at the trunk, without necessarily reaching for the

hands (Fig. 100e). For demonstrating poses such balancing aids are practiced (for example a lunge with arms spread to the side, a scale or a final stand with free arm positioning) (Fig. 100d/e). Such support can be helpful, and necessary for the galleon's figure, or for the mounting of the "chair" (Fig. 100e, also Fig. 90a/b, p. 125).

Fig. 100a-e: Balancing aid for completed figures

Landing aids

Jump downs from people are often done while hand grasping the bottom person who supports and cushions the jump (Fig. 92a/b). Additionally, spotting children can co-control the landing by catching the stomach and by holding the back (Fig. 96, p. 134).

3 Third and Fourth Level: Introduction to the Technique of Spotter Grips

3.1 With Regard to the Methodical Procedure

Because successful spotter actions have a very complex structure, spotter grips and conduct ought *to be learned step by step*. When introducing a new spotter grip the following method can be attempted. Organizational hints are also added for reasons of completion. In the practical situation, hints and partial methodical steps for the acquisition of skills are given at the same time. Inclusion of this area of activity is not possible here for reason of space and because it does not link with the general theme outlined in the introduction.

In conjunction with the theory in chapter A I. 2. (p. 21-24), a general methodical procedure for spotter grips and conduct is first described. Then following this structure, three practical examples are given that demonstrate the approach for practice lessons.

General Methodical Course Within a Lesson

Tune in on spotting and securing

The children run criss-cross through the gym and are given reaction exercises and game types that, at first, awaken their attention. Depending on psycho-social problems and necessities of the group, further chosen tasks to practice cooperation follow (see practical examples, p. 71-110). In any case exercises that help the children to adapt to a partner, as well as to learn easy spotter grips and higher level actions, should be offered repeatedly. These can be given as a transition to the lesson theme at the apparatus.

Description and demonstration of the grip onset

The observing children sit two to three meters away from each other alongside the apparatus, or next to the demonstrating teacher. In as far as ability allows, the teacher provides a first impression by demonstrating the total course of action, and the added spotter grips, in order to be able to structure the following step-by-step learning approach.

The grip onset is demonstrated, described and explained in child-like terms (single words) by the teacher to a non-performing child. Special terms can be clarified here or introduced (example: Clamp grip = clamp around the thighs or upper arm).

Testing and checking the grip contact
The children test the grip contact in small groups (groups of three) with a non-moving, meaning a "completely motionless," person. It's helpful to organise playful tasks after the first test.

Example: Grip contact for a turn grip forward:

The children form a triangle. Two children are spotters and stand facing each other, hands being held on their backs. The third child stands sideways to them and holds his arms far down rearward. Upon call, the spotters turn once around their longitudinal axis, and then quickly place the turn grip forward onto the third child. Thereby the children not only tighten their grip, but the teacher checks how well the children make contact under time pressure.

Explanations of the function and effects of spotter grips
The children come together and the teacher explains the purpose of the spotter grips, demonstrating how they work and formulating a task for testing them.

Testing the effect of spotter grips in small groups
The children test the effect of the newly learned spotter grip in an easy, overseeable, safe situation.

Example for the support grip on the upper arm for a squat vault:

The spotting children lift the gymnast with a support grip during a straight jump.

Example for the turn grip forward:

The spotting children turn the standing gymnast forward so that he has to bow forward.

Tasks for optimization: The child being supported makes a large step with a half turn between the spotting children, and the two spotters must now quickly apply the turn grip on the other side.

The teacher demonstrates the entire spotter action

The children are called together in a common observation spot. The teacher demonstrates the complex spotter actions, with regard to location, spotter grip, spotter conduct, together with a briefly instructed child as co-spotter and a gymnast moving in slow motion. The teacher accompanies the demonstration with easy terminology single words (for example "hands in front," "look at your upper arm!" "Carry him!" and "Hold on").

Feedback through the children: children demonstration

A group of children copy the teacher's demonstration and show if the demonstration was understood. Before the groups reassemble for practice the teacher can correct, demonstrate and accentuate certain points.

Practice and application

The children practice spotting in small groups. The teacher observes, corrects certain spotters and gymnasts and interrupts practice if the majority keeps showing the same mistake. As an additional demonstration he clarifies the not yet understood spotter actions or parts of it. In this case, additional reinforcing tasks should be formulated.

3.2 Practical Lesson Examples for the Introduction of Spotter Grips

With regard to the above mentioned description for the methodical approach, the first example given is the kicking up to handstand until the following roll out of it. Depending on the ability level of the group, it is not necessary to enforce all methodical steps, but one task can be summarized with regard to the given information.

Due to time factors, information reception limits and the motor abilities of the children, the following steps are possible to execute within one lesson. Only in university and coaching seminars can the entire complex be trained for demonstration.

The first steps are suggested for beginners (also with regard to spotting), the following ones for the later lessons.

First Example:
From Handstand front Against the Wall to Handstand Forward Roll in Movement Connection

In order to tune in with the lesson, tasks next to the initial running part, and tasks for support and body tension should be included, preferably as partner exercises.

Handstand, front against the wall

The children are in groups of three, next to each other with one mat each at the wall. The practicing child positions her-/himself rearward to the wall, into squat support, and climbs with the feet up the wall, until he reaches the handstand position (Fig. 101 and photo p. 138).

1. Spotter task

After the demonstration by the teacher the spotters stand sideways next to the gymnast and correct the body posture *verbally* and *through touching*.

Example:

They "tap" the seat with their fingers in order to check the tension and to create awareness. Additionally they can say: "Squeeze your seat!" They point to an arched back or to too strong a hip angle for correction.

Intention: Partner adaptation and learning to see the movement.

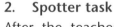

2. Spotter task

After the teacher's demonstration the spotters place *the spotter grips* on a *motionless person*. They reach around a thigh (Fig. 101) and move the gymnast away from the wall, then they lead him back.

Intention: Introduction of the spotter grip in a motionless state for the gymnast.

Fig. 101: Handstand against a wall

3. Spotter task

The gymnast *is lifted* into the vertical position with the above mentioned spotter grip (adjustment of the hip and arm/trunk angle and the arch).

Intention: Demonstrating the spotter function "to carry".

4. Spotter task

The gymnast swings with one leg and pushes away from the wall, closes the legs quickly and the spotters *"grab"* the thighs.

Intention: Application of the spotter grip under accelerated conditions.

5. Spotter task

The practicing child receives *"as much as necessary – as little as possible"* assistance when swinging away from the wall and when standing in handstand. He is only accompanied with "finger tip feeling".

Intention: To learn the ability to accompany a movement.

6. Spotter task

Efficient children can do this exercise on their own. The assisting children stand with widely spread arms, ready to step in and secure the movement, in order *to protect* the child from falling.

Intention: To learn the ability to secure.

Variation: Handstand from prone position on a box

For further reinforcement or repetition one can offer the handstand from a prone position off a box. The gymnast jumps into brief support on the box, lowers to prone position and supports himself downward along the box. Hands are placed approximately two feet from the box onto the floor. The spotter tasks are executed in the same manner as for the wall handstand (Fig. 102). The gymnast is then put back onto the box and lifts himself back up to

Fig. 102: Handstand from a box

143

support. All further exercise tasks are equivalent to the ones suggested for the wall handstand.

Hint:
The same set up can also be used for handstand forward roll (see below).

Kicking up into handstand

1. **Spotter task**

The gymnast is in lunge position in front of a mat with arms up. The spotters stand sideways to the gymnast with their legs straddled on the mat. Both spotters stretch their close hand toward the gymnast. Those hands reach for the thigh (Fig. 103) and lift the legs while swinging up to a handstand. The far hand quickly joins and clamps the thigh from behind. The performing child is being "carried" upward into the handstand. The second hand prevents a fall in case of too much swing. Thus, the spotters "clutch" the thighs at the earliest

Fig. 103: Before handstand

possible moment and accompany the procedure with both hands to establish balance (Fig. 129, p. 169). When the landing leg is brought down the hips need to be held high (the "close" hands can slide into the hip bend in order to keep the center of gravity high if children are experienced) until the landing leg has arrived relatively close to the support base.

Intentions: Getting to know the different functions of the spotter's actions during kick-up to handstand under accelerated conditions, as well as the course of action "going toward – going along – securing the end position" and spotting until the end of the exercise.

2. **Spotter task**

Kicking up to handstand under accelerated conditions. Both spotters reach with their closer hand toward the gymnast and "grab" the thigh at the earliest possible moment, and accompany with both hands until a balanced position is reached (Fig. 129, p. 169).

Intention: Learning the action sequence "going toward – early spotting – supporting" in an accelerated situation.

3.   Spotter task

Kicking up to handstand and spotting assistance "only as much as necessary – as little as possible". Reduce spotting, only one child accompanies the movement.

Intention: Practicing to accompany the movement.

4.   Spotter task

Kicking up to a handstand. One child secures the movement in a passive, but ready to go manner, holding hands in support grip position, or open arms ready to catch, in case of a fall.

Intention: Demonstration the task "securing".

Handstand forward roll
*   from handstand against the wall
*   from a handstand off a box
*   from kicking up to a handstand

Spotter tasks

The spotters reach around the thigh and carry the practicing child into the rolling movement (Fig. 130, p. 170).

Intention: Movement support and steering through spotters.

Movement connection:
Handstand forward roll, straight jump and cat leap
Spotter tasks
*   Reach around thigh during handstand forward roll and steer the movement.
*   Support the straight jump and cat leap movement by lifting the practicing child with the closer hand underneath the armpit, and offering the far hand for support (Fig. 124a-e, p. 167 and Fig. 130, p. 170).

Intentions: Application of different spotter grips with different functions; change of location during spotting; walking along during locomotion; movement steering, support and accompaniment.

Second Example: Pullover on the Bars

The gymnast stands behind the bar, two spotting children stand sideways to the bar facing each other.

The hands are moving in preparation toward the gymnast and reach with the close hand (to the bar) on the upper part of the gymnast's seat, and with the other hand slightly below the seat. Standing close to the gymnast the spotters assist the upward movement of the center of gravity with bent arms for the following pullover (Fig. 104).

Fig. 104: Pullover

1. Spotter task

The gymnast stands with regular grip in front of the bar, one leg held back in preparation for swinging up.

For smaller assisting children it's advisable to start as follows: Both children stand facing each other in front of the bar and reach for their hands in order to determine the distance from each other, and the positioning to the apparatus (sideways). Then they turn the grasped hands in front of the stomach of the gymnast, release the grasp in order to bring the hands behind the seat for carrying (palms of the hand to the seat).

The gymnast swings the swing leg twice in order to get into the rhythm of the movement. On the third swing he performs a pullover with carrying support of the two spotters, who also steer the hips toward the bar. They must "push" until the center of gravity (hips) is on top of the bar.

Intention: Getting to know the location, the spotter grip and the assisting functions.

2. Spotter task

The gymnast performs the pullover a few times in a row while jumping off after having reached a support (through a cast in brief support), and swings up anew. Therefore the spotting children must move toward the gymnast underneath the bar, the helping hands stretch out towards him, and the hands are brought again underneath the seat. Then they carry and guide the center of gravity on top of the bar. For the next run-through the practicing child should immediately bounce off after the landing for the second, third . . . pullover. Now the children must find the grip onsets much faster.

Intentions: Solidifying of a learned spotter grip a few times in a row, in immediate succession. Learning of the fast application of the same spotter grip, and first assisting or accompanying of an exercise sequence (here, for the connection of the same skill).

3. Spotter task

The practicing child performs two to three pullovers and the assisting children accompany the movement with both hands, "touching" the seat according to the principle "As much as necessary – as little as possible". For further tries, only one child accompanies with "finger-tip-feeling".

Intention: Learning the movement accompaniment with "finger-tip-feeling" with regard to timing and level of strength input.

4. Spotter task

For more advanced children it's now only necessary to have one child for securing. The gymnast performs a pullover. The securing child does not move toward the pullover movement anymore, but stands ready with open arms in front of the bar, observes the movement initiation (in order to assess success) and the further course of the movement, and, in an "emergency", assists the gymnast with the newly learned spotter grip.

5. Spotter task

The gymnast performs a movement sequence with two, differently executed spotter grips that are to be set on subsequently (Fig. 105.1-105.6).

- Pullover to support (1, 2), cast (3) and landing with immediate push-off to jump down (4) to a second pullover (5) (Spotting/movement accompaniment or securing, according to needs, as described above) and jump down.

Fig. 105.1-105.6: Movement connection: Pullover, Jump down, 2nd pullover, Under-swing

• Run through "hang-stand" with release of the hands or under-swing from stand (6) (depending on the child's ability). The spotting children are two feet away from the bar. The gymnast finishes the final part of the movement and the spotters move close to the approaching body. The close, helping hands "get" the back in order to prevent a falling back, and to assist the rise into the stand. The far hands go in front of the stomach and prevent a fall forward. The spotters can be told in a simplified way to "catch" the gymnast (Fig. 105.6).

Intention: Application of the newly learned spotter grip twice in a row in combination with another spotter grip and change of location.

Third Example:
Support Grip for a Squat Vault Over a Box

First section: Introduction without vault apparatus on the spot, in an overseeable and safe situation

Groups of three are formed for the following tasks. Per exercise, each child is once the gymnast, once spotter on the right and then on the left.

1. Spotter task
The two assisting children stand facing the gymnast who bounces in succession twice on the spot and finishes with a high jump (tight take-off). Arms remain low for the grip onset that will follow. The assisting children attempt to adapt to the movement of the gymnast through copying the jumps mirror-like. Then they change roles.

Intention: Tuning in to the gymnast and his course of movement, and adaptation of both spotters.

2. Spotter task
The teacher or coach demonstrates and explains the grip onset with a child. In groups of three two check out the grip on the standing child.

Intention: Introduction of the spotter grip "support grip" (clamp grip) with a motionless person who is going to be spotted later on (Fig. 106).

Fig. 106: Support grip

3. Spotter task

The assisting children reach around the upper arms of the gymnast in support grip, and lift him, after two bounces on the spot with the third a strong take-off, high overhead to the best of their abilities.

Intention: Adaptation to the gymnast, the course of the movement and to the spotting child. Being aware of the function "carrying" with support grip.

4. Spotter task

After the teacher's demonstration and explanation of the following new focal points with an assisting child and a gymnast, the children once again reach around the upper arm in support grip, go with bent arms very close to the jumper and repeat the task as before. They now stem the jumper energetically upward close to their own bodies through the extension of their arms with support grip (Fig. 107).

Intention: Demonstrating how to best "carry" with support grip when close to the gymnast, and the energetic strength input during support.

Fig. 107: Stem him upward

5. Spotter task

The spotting children stand shoulder to shoulder in front of the jumping child in a step position (inner leg in front) and reach again, with the "inner" helping hand, underneath the armpit (inner side of the upper arm), and with the "outer" hand to the outer part of the arm. With take-off for the third high jump, the spotters pull the jumper toward them and lift him up again. This is at first demonstrated by a group of three, and later by all participants.

Intention: Getting to know the latter position on the box, and how to get into the position "shoulder lock" (Fig. 108).

Fig. 108: Shoulder lock

6. Spotter task

The assisting children now support the gymnast with the learned spotter grip, out of a small run with hurdle step, based on what they have learned so far ("shoulder lock"). For this they need to establish eye contact with the jumping child who is approximately nine feet away, and stretch their hands in ready-to-go support grip toward him. During the hurdle step, just prior to take-off, the spotters "grasp" the upper arms in support grip and pull the jumping child toward them in order to lift him up. This is first demonstrated in a group of three before all others can go ahead and start practicing.

Intention: Getting to know the aspects of "going toward" and "early, quick reaching in" for an accelerated course of movement.

7. Spotter task

The assisting children now support the gymnast out of a small run and hurdle step to take-off with the learned spotter grip and conduct ("shoulder lock"). *A new addition* is that they make *fast, small steps, backward* with the airborne child (without frontal changes). The inner leg goes back first when walking backward.

8. Spotter task

Variation with spring board:

The assisting children stand on a long mat with a spring board in front. A third child starts running with medium speed with arms in low position and performs a straight jump. The spotting children are shoulder to shoulder behind the spring board with their hands toward the gymnast, they catch him in support grip and carry the airborne gymnast three feet backward to a landing on the mat. Only when the landing is completed is the support grip released (Fig. 109).

Intention: Applying the entire assisting action complex into a dynamic, yet hazard-free exercise situation, and being aware of holding on to the gymnast until he arrives in a secure stand.

Fig. 109: Catch him in support grip

**Second part: Introduction to "vaulting apparatus"
in an overseeable and safe situation**

Tasks at the long box (spotting blocks or stacked panel mats)

9. Spotter task

A spring board is placed in front of a long box. The spotting children are standing sideways, the "box leg" placed in front toward the front of the box. The gymnast stands on the spring board and supports the hands on the box. The assisting children reach around the upper arms (still gently in order not to disturb the initial movement) in support grip. The gymnast bounces twice and gets ready to jump on three to kneel or squat on, depending on the ability. The helping hands carry the child onto the box. The gymnast rises up and walks to the end of the box and jumps off onto a mat with good landing control as a preparation for the second flight phase.

Tip:

Two more children can assist with the landing of the straight jump dismount on the front and back (intensifying activity).

Intention: Becoming aware of the skill specific movement support and guiding at the apparatus in a slowed down situation.

10. Spotter task

The gymnast jumps onto the box and kneels down, or squats on from a run. The assisting children are sideways at the front of the box, the leg close to the box in front. Hands reach toward the oncoming gymnast in support grip manner and "catch" the upper arms with the beginning of the support on

Fig. 110: "Catch" the upper arms!

the box, and carry the child onto it. (Fig. 110) The long box adds additional security in case the spotters fail to keep the gymnast from falling forward, due to its padding and extra space.

Intention: Creating awareness of the skill specific action sequence of the first flight phase in a secured situation.

11. Spotter task

After the squat on, the gymnast puts the hands a little further in front and squats forward in support until he reaches the end of the box. Two more spotters (or the same children having quickly run to the end of the box) stand shoulder to shoulder, the inner leg in front, and reach around the upper arms of the gymnast who now squats off the box like a "parcel (tight tuck)". The spotting children carry the gymnast off the box.

Intention: Getting to know the spotter task in the second flight phase for same spotters (see above) in combination with spotter tasks for the first flight and support phase, even though it's timely separated (Fig. 111).

Fig. 111: Support grip

Tasks at the side box: Squat on and off
12. Spotter task

The children stand behind the box, hands in preparation for applying the support grip, establishing eye contact with the gymnast who is getting ready to run. He runs and jumps to squat on. The assisting children try to quickly "grasp" the upper arms. With the rising and jumping off they secure the landing at the back and front ("sandwich").

Intention: Learning to reach in quickly with support grip, with over-the-box-reaching of the arms.

13. Spotter task

The children stand shoulder to shoulder behind the box, hands ready for applying the support grip, and eyes in contact with the gymnast. The gymnast squats on from a run. The spotting children quickly reach around the upper arms and keep holding on. From a squat stand the gymnast squats off (like a parcel) with a small supported jump (Fig. 112.1-112.3). The spotters carry the "parcel" from the box while walking backward. They keep holding on to the arms until the gymnast has completed his landing and the legs are back on the floor (Fig. 112.2).

Intention: Consciously looking for the location where shoulder lock occurs (in order to avoid a falling through). Experiencing the function of carrying the gymnast in the second flight phase and to keep holding on until a secure landing is reached.

Fig. 112.1-112.3: Carrying the gymnast in the 2nd flight phase

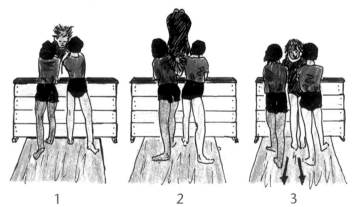

Fig. 113.1-113.3: Going shoulder to shoulder backward

14. Spotter task

The children stand shoulder to shoulder behind the box, hands ready for the support grip, eyes establishing contact with the gymnast. The gymnasts squat on and off rapidly out of a run. The assisting children grasp fast in support grip and guide the children over the box. With the landing they erect the upper body and keep holding the arm until the child has landed safely.

Intention: Application in an accelerated situation, getting to know the rise in the second flight phase and holding on until a secure landing is reached (Fig. 113.1-113.3).

15. Spotter task

The children repeat the squat on and off from a run. Depending on the abilities of the children one can now move toward a movement accompaniment following the principle "as much as necessary – as little as possible". The teacher should determine readiness for securing only for the more advanced children (hands are ready to reach in support grip for upper arms, close to the arms, or landing security on front and back) (Fig. 114).

Intention: Acquiring the action ability to accompany movement and to secure (Fig. 115).

Spotting, movement accompaniment and securing for a squat vault over a box

16. Spotter task

The gymnast performs a squat vault from a run. The spotting children stand again with shoulder lock behind the box, establish eye contact, stretch their arms in support grip manner toward the gymnast, grasp quickly during take-off around the upper arms, lift the vaulter over the box, stand him up while walking along backward (inner leg first).

Intention: Applying the entire movement supporting action sequence for spotting a squat vault.

17. Spotter task

The children repeat the squat vault and the spotting children try to assist the secure vaulters only with finger tip feeling. The principle "as much as necessary – as little as possible" applies where the movement seems to show mistakes (for example, if the chest doesn't rise in the second flight phase). Then, they form a lane and repeat their actions for the same task.

Intention: Applying movement accompaniment for the squat vault with a widened spotter lane, as transfer to securing (Fig. 114).

18. Spotter task

The children repeat the squat vault, and the spotting children try only to secure those that are already very skilled at it. For this they form a lane, two

feet wide, standing sideways. After the support they stretch out their arms towards the gymnast. They secure the landing with the hand close to the box going behind the back ("picking up and lifting" in case of falling back), and with the hand far from the box in front of the stomach (not at the hips, because it causes bending), in order to prevent a falling forward.

Fig. 114: "Sandwich-grip"

Increasingly the securing hands are only held in preparation in order to be able to reach in ("sandwich") and catch the gymnast (Fig. 114). Finally, only one spotter secures (Fig. 115).

Fig. 115: Security

Intention: To secure movement of the squat vault.

Hints for the application of listed spotter tasks

- Almost all listed methodical steps for the learning of the spotter grip, "support grip", can be applied to skills, like pike-ons or pike vault and straddle on or straddle vault.
- The above described 18 spotter tasks are undertaken in different lessons. A finished complex should always be offered (for example, jumping onto the long box, or squat on and off the side box, or squat vault over the box).
- In further lessons the straddle vault (also over a buck, see Fig. 154, p. 182) and the pike vault (Fig. 155, p. 183) can be worked on in similar ways with chosen spotter tasks.

Application in the Apparatus Circuit "Low Bar – Floor – Vault"

With the application of the exercise connections so far learned, the spotter grips and conduct are learned over again, trained, confirmed and made applicable. The children must continually change the spotter grips and location. Thus, they reach an exceptionally high standard of spotting.

Described in keywords, the following shows an apparatus circuit that includes three of the learned spotter grips. In addition, the choreographic creation of the cooperation is included. At the end of the lesson the learned material can be demonstrated at various parallel stations, together with music, and can turn into a success for all participants (for example to "Take five" and "Trolly song" from Dave Brubeck or "Wheel of fortune" and "All that she wants" from ACE OF BASE or "Macarena" from LOS DEL RIO).

Course of exercise and spotter actions
in an exercise combination (Fig. 116.1-116.14)

- Pullover: Both hands support underneath the seat (Fig. 116.1).
- Back hip circle: Both hands go quickly under the bar (Fig. 116.2) and support under the seat (Fig. 116.3).

Fig. 116.1-116.3: Pullover, back hip circle

- Under-swing from standing position: The spotters are roughly two feet away from the bar (Fig. 116.4), and secure the landing by "forking" stomach and back (Fig. 116.5).

Fig. 116.4-116.6: Under-swing, landing, hops

Fig. 116.7-116.9: Handstand, roll

- Forward hops to the mat: The spotters move simultaneously in side steps to the jumping child (Fig. 116.6).

- Handstand forward roll, straight jump: The spotters quickly stand on the mat (Fig. 116.7) and reach around the thighs, while the gymnast kicks up to handstand (Fig. 116.8), accompany the forward roll (Fig. 116.9), and secure stomach and back after the straight jump (Fig. 116.10) (this serves as an exercise for the spotters), or help with the rising part with a grip of the close hand under the armpit and the far hand at the hand of the gymnast (Fig. 99, p. 136 and Fig. 124b, p. 167).

Fig. 116.10-116.11: Straight jump, cat leaps

- Run and cat leap: The spotters are synchronized (support with one hand under the armpit and the other under the hand of the jumping child) (Fig. 124 a-e, p. 167 or without spotting: Fig. 116.11).

- Run hurdle step cartwheel: The spotting children perform cartwheels alongside the vault (Fig. 116.12), and run behind the box/vault to assist with support grip, while the middle child has performed a cartwheel backward out of a run and turns away with a half turn in order to gain space for the run to the vault.

12   13   14

Fig. 116.12-116.14: Cartwheel, squat vault, pose

- Squat vault (straddle or pike vault): The gymnast runs to perform a support vault and the spotting children support in support grip until the landing is secured (Fig. 116.13).

- "Finishing pose": The group of three terminates the exercise combination in a freely created, agreed upon, "final pose" (Fig. 116.14).

4 SECURING

Securing means to observe attentively, to think and to move. Signals of readiness need to be shown by the participants through eye contact with the gymnast and readily held hands. Over and over, the teacher needs to make the spotters aware of their responsibility for the safety of the other. Misconduct should be criticized constructively by the teacher and the other students. Unskilled spotters tend to move away instinctively from the approaching body of the gymnast when erroneous movements suddenly occur. They step back, instead of moving supportingly toward the gymnast. They usually show concern about their conduct afterwards. This spontaneous stepping aside can be eliminated if the teacher hints early toward possible problems of the movement that needs to be secured, and by allowing "securing" to be specifically practiced consciously through the proper spotting levels, and learned through the ability of movement accompaniment.

Games

In preparation for good reaction and action abilities for securing, "in case of a fall", one can start the lesson with a game.

Mannequins!
At first the students run freely in the gym. Upon call of the teacher "mannequins", they freeze on the spot (reaction ability, balance ability, body tension).

As an extension of the task the students slide after the "freeze part" slowly to the floor ("as if they let the air out"). The children lie relaxed and sluggish on the floor. The teacher checks this on some children by lifting an arm that should fall right back to the floor.

Variation:
Robot (let fall, because the robot's batteries are empty).

After this introductory game has been played 5 to 6 times, one can, as an extension, directly start to prepare for "securing" with the following small "rescue game".

Secret number falls! Rescue him!

Each student selects a number between one and ten and keeps it to himself. In a limited space (for example the volleyball field or floor area) the children run criss-cross. The teacher calls a number. Those that have chosen this number freeze briefly, and then let themselves glide to the floor very slowly "in slow motion". The other children must try to catch them before they have sunken completely to the ground.

Balance Apparatus

A first introduction into the securing conduct is learned when the children accompany another child over a balance apparatus (rounded beam, beam, rope). When the child balances forward, a second child goes

- at first, helping through hand holding (Fig. 117)

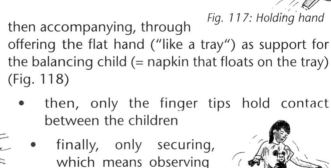

Fig. 117: Holding hand

- then accompanying, through offering the flat hand ("like a tray") as support for the balancing child (= napkin that floats on the tray) (Fig. 118)

- then, only the finger tips hold contact between the children

- finally, only securing, which means observing and waiting. The arms can be held toward the gymnast as a sign of readiness (Fig. 119).

Fig. 118: Offering hand

For jump downs, just like for vaulting, the landings are secured by putting the hands on the stomach and back (Fig. 120, 121, p. 162).

Fig. 119

Different Apparatus

As described in the previous chapters, securing is a waiting, observing behavior during an entire course of a movement, in order to reach in if necessary. In the first securing situations the children need to be told what could happen as a possible problem during certain skills. The children must then talk about what they intend to do in such cases. The teacher must, in case of a failed attempt, describe the rescuing action.

Fig. 120: Securing landing

Securing behavior can, as a "non-emergency-situation", be schooled on the floor and other equipment, if, for landings after a straight jump or a jump down, the landing child is secured with the spotter's close hand behind the back and the other hand on the front, "forking" or "sandwich".

"Catching Big Macs"

At first they still reach around the body. They can be instructed, in a game like fashion, to imagine the picture of a sandwich or a "Big Mac", where the helping hands are the buns and the flying and landing child is the meat that must be caught." Who slips through?" (Fig. 121).

Increasingly the catching children touch the gymnast's body less and less, and finally not at all.

Fig. 121: "Sandwich"

Examples for securing landings on the floor

*   Two bounces on the spot and a straight jump to a safe landing in motionless position.
*   One or two legged take-off to a straight jump.
*   Roll forward with immediate straight jump.
*   Roll backward with subsequent straight jump.
*   Round-off intermediate bounce and straight jump to stand.

Examples for securing landings from the bar

- Under-swing (Fig. 122).

- Cast to brief support and jump down.

- Forward downward roll from support to hang and jump off.

- Swinging in long hang.

- Jump to long hang on a high bar.

Fig. 122: Under-swing and "sandwich" grip

Vaulting equipment

- Jump-downs or straight jumps off a box.

- Landing after a squat on from the long box.

- Landing after various support jumps.

II. Spotter Grips and Conduct

In this section all spotter grips and conduct for all essential skills will be described – structured according to apparatus groups. Differentiation is being made for spotting that the children can do on their own, and spotting that should only be done by the teacher.

Regarding the terms "close" and "far" spotter hand

For a better practical understanding with regard to explanations of spotter grips, we speak about the far and the close hand. One assumes this is in relation to starting from a standing position where the side of the spotter's body points toward the gymnast or the apparatus. Therefore, one helping hand is close to the gymnast or apparatus, the other one is away from it (Fig. 124a-e, p. 167, 129, p. 169, 172, p. 195 and see photo on the opposite page.) In the following examples they are referred to as hand closest to the body or apparatus and hand farthest from the body or apparatus.

Illustrated explanation of the spotter grips

"Just like" pictorial speech is helpful for movement learning ("make yourself small like a package", "Roll like a ball"), this should also be used for spotting. It is remarkable how this helps children to remember spotting actions.

Examples:

When a close hand lifts or supports the gymnast with the palm of the hand, a hand signalling "Please, it's your turn!" can be given as a reminder. When explaining the spotter grip for a kick up to handstand the teacher can say, for example: "Stretch the hand that is close to the gymnast toward him, and make a hand movement as if you want to say: 'Please ...!'". The palm of the hand can now be placed on the thigh for lifting (Fig. 129, p. 169).

With this first hand movement close to the body, almost all carrying spotter grips are introduced: Skills like pullover, back hip circle, kick to handstand, front and back handsprings, front and back flips, as well as the forward roll on beam, are examples for this.

Further examples for pictorial basic terms, like "crocodile grip" ("... and the crocodile snaps its jaws!") for turn grip, or "throw out the anchor" for cupping the hand on the shoulder, in order to secure landings after handsprings, are illustrated in the following text.

Degree of difficulty

Skills of completely different standards are being listed, because the compulsory exercises that are done in gymnastics clubs can only be offered in schools for higher classes, or not at all.

Later on stars are given for the different degrees of difficulty – taking spotting into consideration.

*	For beginners: easy gymnastics skills, simple or no spotting.
**	For children with some experience: more sophisticated skills and spotting.
***	For advanced gymnasts and spotters.
****	For very skilled gymnasts and spotters.

1   FLOOR EXERCISE

Straight Jump *

- From a squat stand: Two spotters stand shoulder to shoulder in front of the gymnast, the inner hand goes under the armpit and supports it, the outer hand grasps the wrist (see Fig. 99, p. 136 and Fig. 123.1).

- From a stand: Two spotters stand shoulder to shoulder in front of the jumper, the inner hand goes under the armpit, the outer hand reaches around the upper arm in support grip. The jumper bounces twice on the spot. For the third, strong jump he is carried up in the air (Fig. 123.1, 123.2).

- Out of and in locomotion: Two spotters stand next to the gymnast, reach with the inner, closer hand under the armpit, the outer, far hand is held in preparation for support of the partner. The spotters run with the gymnast (Fig. 124) and lift him with take-off up in the air (Fig. 124b-e).

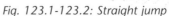

Fig. 123.1-123.2: Straight jump

Cat Leap (Fig. 124c), Scissor Leap (Fig. 124d) *, Stride and Split Leap (Fig. 124e) **

Same spotter grips apply here as for the straight jump.

a

b

c

d

e

Fig. 124a-e: Supporting leaps

Forward Roll *

The actual forward roll *should not be spotted by the children*, because, if for example, they push at the seat when rolling back, the body might push down onto the neck vertebrae. This is not acceptable from a health standpoint. For children that do not succeed in rolling over their head *the teacher* can reach from in front with both hands for the gymnast's hips, and thus lift the seat over the head in order to initiate the rolling movement (Fig. 125).

Fig. 125

167

Spotting of the children as a preparatory exercise for the introduction of the rolling movement:

In order to demonstrate the support phase, the carrying into the rolling movement and the extending of the legs, two spotters can hold the gymnast's feet in high squat support. They stand shoulder to shoulder behind the practicing student and lift him, through reaching around the ankles, into the free squat support (remain well tucked!). By extending the legs and bending the arms the gymnast starts to roll forward (Fig. 126 and photo p. 102).

Fig. 126: Forward roll

Backward Roll **

For the same reasons as for the forward roll, spotting of the children amongst themselves is not appropriate.

For weaker children that are not succeeding with the overhead rolling, the teacher can help with both hands from behind by lifting their hips overhead in order to initiate the rolling movement (Fig. 127).

Fig. 127: Backward roll

Hint:
If the backward roll is being practiced on a two part box, two children can stand next to the box and reach with both hands, a doubled rope or bicycle inner tube (see photo p. 26) under the stomach of the gymnast and lift the seat (center of gravity) over the support location or the head. This enables the extension of the arms. The gymnast must maintain a tightly tucked position throughout (Fig. 128).

Fig. 128: Backward roll on elevation

Headstand **

The gymnast goes into a squat support and places head and hands as a three-point-triangle on the mat. One or two children stand at the same height, sideways, next to him, and reach for the legs that are still tucked, while reaching around the thighs. For this they need to counter-turn their hands (as for the turn grip forward/"crocodile grip", see Fig. 160, p. 185 and 171, p. 193).

With the extension of the legs they hold the gymnast with support grip in the vertical.

Kick Up to Handstand **

Two spotting children stand at a right angle forward and to the side of the gymnast. The close hand points with the palm of the hand upward (gesture: "Please, it's your turn!", see photo p. 164) and goes towards the thigh of the gymnast (Fig. 129), in order to support the up-swing of the leg from the beginning, in a lifting manner. The spotter's far hand grasps the thigh in vertically from behind as quickly as possible, and thus secures him from falling over. In the subsequent course of the exercise the spotting turns into assistance for balance with "finger tip feeling".

Fig. 129: Kick up to handstand

Handstand Forward Roll **

Two spotters reach for the thighs, just as described for the kick up to handstand (Fig. 130.1). With the onset for the rolling movement the spotters lead the handstand past the vertical and carry the gymnast slowly into the rolling movement (Fig. 130.2). They prevent a falling over with straight hips, as well as folding together with strongly bent hips, by holding the child and leading him into a slight hip bend.

Fig. 130.1-130.2: Handstand, forward roll

Advancement of spotting

After the rolling down, or for the following straight jump (Fig. 131.1), the spotters help the gymnast up to a stand by moving along in the direction of the movement. The close hand under the armpit lifts the gymnast up, and the far hand is offered to the gymnast for support (Fig. 131.2). This spotter grip should at first be practiced from a squat sit.

Fig. 131.1-131.2

Fig. 132.1-132.2

Backward Roll to Handstand **

When the gymnast starts rolling back the spotters attempt to reach for the thighs at the earliest possible moment (Fig. 80a). From the beginning, the spotters must be at shoulder height to the gymnast and pull him into the vertical (Fig. 132.1-132.2).

Hint:

The spotter grip is easy to practice when rolling back to a candle stick position. During the extension to the candle stick the spotters must quickly reach for the thighs.

Cartwheel **

Children should not spot cartwheels because the chance for injury is significant (for example feet could smack the spotter in the face). A subject specific method (starting from the scissors handstand) with orientation aids (floor markings, rope, rubber hands) is sufficient for the learning of this skill.

Round-off **

The round-off, being performed on the floor, is similar to the cartwheel, in that it's important not to have the children spot each other, because, here too, one runs into the possibility of injury (see above).

Hint:

If the round-off, as part of preparatory exercises, is being practiced *from an elevation*, for example bench, declining mat or something similar, two spotters can reach around the hips from behind and guide the movement into the vertical position (Fig. 133.1), maintain balance in the handstand phase (Fig. 133.2), and turn the body around its longitudinal axis for

Fig. 133.1-133.3: Handstand rotation for round-off

Fig. 134.1-134.2: Round-off, 2nd phase

landing (Fig. 133.3). For heavier children the teacher is, at first, one of the two spotters. With acceleration of the round-off movement only one child spots with both hands at the hips (Fig. 134.1-134.2).

Round-off for the advanced:
If the round-off is being performed dynamically, one or two spotters can reach for the landing with the close hand underneath the center of gravity (seat), in order to carry the body for a subsequent straight jump, and with the far hand they support against the body (shoulder girdle = long lever for the force onset) in order to stop a backward rotation of the body.

Front Handspring Including Front Walk-over and Front Handspring Stepout ***

Principal spotter grip

The spotters form a lane in front of the gymnast. If the front handspring is performed slowly the spotting children kneel (Fig. 135). With increased ability, and done from a hurdle, the front handspring is spotted and steered to standing position (see photo p. 173).

- The hand close to the body points with the palm of the hand upward (hand gesture: "Please, it's your turn!") and goes toward the gymnast. Then it is placed between upper arm and neck on the shoulder (Fig. 135a/b) in order to lift the gymnast from the floor, and thereafter to erect the upper body (Fig. 136). It may slide further forward during landing and "hook on" to the shoulder

Fig. 135a/b: Spotter grip for front handspring

(= "throw out the anchor") (Fig. 136.2). This prevents a fall forward. This can be the case when the front handspring is done from elevations.

- The far hand of the body goes under the center of gravity (= seat) (Fig. 135a/b) and lifts the body's center during the onset of the movement, in order to then sink down again, with the erection of the upper body. This simultaneously offers a support point as resistive force for the erection of the upper body for the landing (Fig. 136, photo p. 21).

If the front handspring results in falling over forward (for example from elevations), this "seat hand" changes to the upper arm and reaches around it from the front. With the clamping of both hands now, the upper body can best be kept erect. Because of the complexity of these spotter actions they can only be executed by the teacher or coach and advanced students (Fig. 136.3).

Fig. 136: Front handspring: grip for secure landing

Hint:

A support in the lumbar region with the far hand is not acceptable, because

- it increases hyperlordosis (arched back)

- the frequent force impacts of the spotters' hands into the arched back are not healthy

- the support point thus lies above the center of gravity, and therefore does not allow for best carrying, nor can a resistive force be created for the erection of the upper body.

Slow motion front handspring

If the front handspring is performed slowly from a kick up to handstand, the spotters reach with the far arm around the seat in order to carry the well-tightened gymnast through the handstand to a stand (Fig. 137).

Movement accompaniment/movement securing

If the front handspring is performed virtually alone, the hand close to the body only pushes a little bit under the shoulder to help erect the upper body.

Fig. 137: Carrying through handstand

Back Handspring: Flic-flac and Back Handspring Step-out, Back Walk-over and Valdez ****

Basic spotter grip

The spotters form a lane in front of the gymnast. If the back handspring is done from a standing position the spotters kneel down (Fig. 138).

Both hands go toward the center of gravity (= seat) (Fig. 138, 139), the fingers point to the opposite partner. The close hand goes more toward the thigh, lifts the body and supports the rotation. The far hand is placed slightly above the seat and carries the body in the flight phase. It's advantageous to reach with the far hand from above onto the waist of the pants to pull the gymnast into the "sitting position" (Fig. 140). Once the gymnast is airborne one can then carry on the "fist".

Fig. 138: Spotter kneel down

Fig. 139: Flic-flac

Fig. 140: Pulling into seat position

With increasing ability and done out of a round-off, the flic-flac is spotted and guided in standing position (Fig. 141).

Hint:

A support at the shoulder girdle during the flic-flac is not acceptable, because, for one thing, the gymnast can only be carried with one hand – the close one – (which is not executable for young gymnasts) and it counteracts the technical criteria to quickly force the upper body backward into the vertical to a handstand.

Fig. 141: Manual guiding flic-flac

"Slow motion back handspring" *

a) Spotting while lowering backward into a handstand from a high box/mat

The gymnast sits on a mat or box at "stomach height". The spotting children stand, forming a lane, behind the gymnast and put the close arm onto the hips of the sitting child in order to

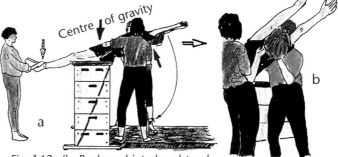

Fig. 142a/b: Backward into handstand

press the center of gravity against the sitting surface during the onset of the movement (Fig. 142a). The far hand goes between upper arm and neck (Fig. 142b) onto the shoulder in order to carry the body down when lowering, and to keep the body up when support is established. Once the hands are placed on the floor the spotter hands go to the thighs, in order to lift the gymnast to a handstand.

Hint:

Teachers and experienced spotters can also grasp from the front (instead of from the shoulder girdle, as described above) between neck and upper arm onto the shoulder when lowering down. Especially for children that are weak in support, the support can be facilitated through keeping the body up by "cupping" the shoulder.

b) Spotting to lower backward into a handstand with partner support

The following way of spotting is not suitable for the dynamic flic-flac (spotters run the chance of injury to the head because of back swinging arms).

The gymnast stands stiffly in front of the spotter lane. The spotters reach for each other's hands. The close grasped hands go toward the thigh and lever the practicing child (not aiming at the center of gravity) from the floor. The far grasped hands move toward the shoulder blades (not into the arch) (Fig. 143.1) and carry the upper body until the straight arms reach support on the floor (Fig. 143.2, 143.3). While lowering the far hands, the close hands must simultaneously lift the thighs of the gymnast in order to place him into a handstand. Both hands reach around the thigh in handstand. (Fig. 143.4).

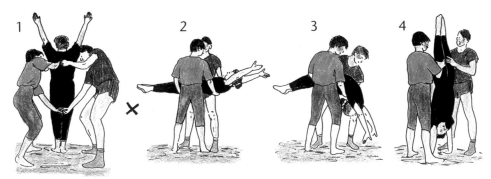

Fig. 143.1-143.4

Spotting variation and spotting for *slowly* executed flic-flac and back handspring step-out (Menichelli): The far arms can – especially for faster motion – also reach around the upper body. The close hands go underneath the seat (Fig. 144). For a fast executed flic-flac see Fig. 177, p. 199.

Hint:

The arms of the practicing child must be swung close by the head in order not to hit the spotters.

Side Aerial ****

Teacher spotting: The spotter stands on the side of the forward leg and goes with the close hand into the hip bend of the close hip, in order to lift the

Fig. 144: Slow motion flic-flac

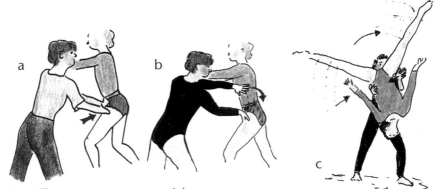

Fig. 145a-c: Three ways to spot an aerial

center of gravity (Fig. 145b). The far spotter hand reaches over the back of the gymnast to the other hip (Fig. 145b) in order to support the longitudinal turn, and to keep the body, under the center of gravity, lifted for landing after the rotation. (Fig. 145c)

Variation:

Older children can support each other (especially when done from a low elevation) by reaching with both hands, or with the lower arm of the close hand into the hip bend, right when the preparatory step is initiated.

Front Aerial ****

Preparatory exercise: Three children stand, with hands extended, next to each other. After two or three common preparatory steps, or an initial hurdle step of the gymnast, the spotters go with a quarter rotation ahead of the movement. The gymnast lowers the upper body for the aerial and the spotters go with the outer, still free hands, under the shoulder, in order to carry (between upper arm and neck, palm of the hand points upward, thumb points to the head of the gymnast).

Hint:

Don't lift shoulder too high (see below).

Spotting from a knee stand: Older children can spot each other by keeping the shoulder girdle with both hands at a certain point during the aerial. The "cupped" hands are offered to the gymnast to put his shoulders into him at thigh height, or they can also reach for the side spread arms at the upper arm. Preferably, it should be done from a low elevation.

Hint:

The shoulder girdle should not be kept too high, because it is then difficult to move the center of gravity over the vertical.

Spotting reduction: As for the side aerial, one experienced spotter stands on the forward leg side and lifts the center of gravity with the close hand during the onset of the movement. The far hand is placed on the back and supports the rotation (see Fig. 145b).

Variation:

An experienced spotter stands on the leg swing side and supports the rotational upward movement energetically with the close hand under the thigh of the swinging leg.

Accompanying spot: An experienced spotter helps the gymnast into a stand during landing with the far hand and long lever arm under/behind the back.

Salto Forward/Somersault (Front Flip) ***/****

Because the front flip is being introduced with equipment aids, and the spotting is of importance primarily in the preparatory steps, the guiding spotter grips can be looked up in those sections. With the take-off from a board we apply the spotter grip with the close hand at the stomach and the far hand at the back (Fig. 146).

Spotting reduction: With the introduction of the flip the close hand turns in anticipation with the

Fig. 146: Front flip

palm of the hand onto the back of the gymnast, now flipping overhead, and supports the transversal rotation as well as bringing the body to a stand. With the landing the far hand goes to the stomach, in order to prevent

Fig. 147: Front flip with rotation support a fall forward ("sandwich") (Fig. 147).

Salto Backward (Back Flip) ****
(Turning Over Backward **: Turn Grip Backward)

The back flip is learned through turning over backward (compare also exercises on the mini-tramp, p. 191-199).

Spotter grips for the back flip ****

Two spotters stand behind the gymnast, extend the close arm toward him and go under the seat, close to the thigh, with the palm of the hand turned toward the gymnast (hand gesture "Please, it's your turn!"). Thus, the gymnast can be lifted, and rotation can be initiated. The second, far hand, supports through pressure under the seat, close to the back (Fig. 93a). When the back flip is performed from standing position (for example from a

Fig. 148: Back flip

slight elevation), it is helpful to reach with this far hand from above into the waist band of the gymnast's shorts, and to carry/pull him away from the starting location (Fig. 149). When the gymnast is overhead he can be carried on the fist. You can also support with a grip at an inner tube which is around the gymnast's body.

Fig. 149: Special grip

Variation for securing the landing:

Shortly before the landing experienced spotters can change hands in order to secure it. The far hand goes behind the back and the close hand in front of the stomach ("sandwich", see Fig. 121, p. 162). This is then, later on, the "proper" securing of the landing, without previous interference with the course of the movement, as is described in the following.

Safety spot for salto backwards ****

If the gymnast can perform the back flip safely with a spot, only the landing needs to be secured. Two spotting children stand opposite each other within two feet distance. They wait for the rotation of the salto, and with the opening for the landing, place the close hand on the stomach in order to prevent the gymnast from falling forward. The far hand goes to the back in order to prevent the gymnast from falling backwards.

2 Vaulting Apparatus for Supported Vaults

(Small and Large Boxes or Stacked Panel Mats, Vaulting Horse)

Kneel On *, Squat On *, Squat Vault **

Spotter grip: Support grip at the upper arm (Fig. 150)

With the spotters in front of the gymnast the inner hand goes under the armpit, and the outer hand reaches around the upper arm.

Spotter conduct: Two spotters stand shoulder to shoulder (shoulder lock) in step position behind the box, the inner leg is placed in front (Fig. 151.1). When the gymnast gains support, the hands of the spotters go toward the arms of the

Fig. 150: Support grip

gymnast and reach around each upper arm (Fig. 150, 151.2). The inner hand is underneath the armpit. At first the spotters prevent the gymnast from falling over (see Fig. 155) or backwards. In the following course of the movement the spotters carry the gymnast from/over the box (Fig. 151.3), raise the upper body and secure the landing (Fig. 151.4). During the course of the exercise they need to take one to two steps backward, starting with the inner leg.

1   2   3   4

Fig. 151.1-151.4: Squat vault: spotting with support grip

Securing:

- If the course of the exercise is increasingly mastered the spotters stand "opened up", this means at a right angle to the box, and grab the upper arm with support grip, until the landing is secured (Fig. 152).

Fig. 152: Squat vault

- Securing the landing: The last step is securing the landing of the gymnast. This happens at the front and back, at first with two, and then, finally, only with one safety spotter. This prevents a falling backward onto the box, as well as tilting forward.

After two spotters have secured the vaulter, the safe vaulter can now be secured with only one spotter from the side (Fig. 153).

(For the squat vault see also the methodical introduction of spotter grips on p. 141-156)

Fig. 153: Securing landing

Straddle On *, Straddle Vault ** and Pike Vault ****

The straddle vault (Fig. 154, 156) and the pike vault (Fig. 155) are supported and guided like the squat vault, with two children spotting in support grip, and in the beginning, with above described "shoulder lock".

Hint:

When the straddle vault is performed over a buck (= a shortened long horse) that is continuously heightened, the teacher stands right in front of

Fig. 154: Straddle and "shoulder lock"

the end of the buck and reaches for both upper arms in order to erect the upper body prior to landing (Fig. 156). In the meantime this can be practiced over a low buck horse or box with assistance from the children (Fig. 154).

Fig. 155: Pike and "shoulder lock"

Fig. 156: Straddle and teacher spot

Tucked Wende Onto and Over the Box *

Children do not have to spot here because the two different activities of the hands, and the associated spotting functions, are too complex, especially since one hand at the center of gravity cannot provide enough force to turn and push. For weaker children, the teacher stands in front of the box, next to the spring board, and supports the upper arm of the gymnast with the close hand (resistive force for the spotter activity of the second hand) and gives a turn-push-aid at the seat/thigh (Fig. 157, see photo page 180).

Fig. 157: Tucked wende

Fencer Vaults *

Children do not spot each other, for the same reasons as for the tucked wende.

Exceptions – in case of repeatedly failed attempts the teacher can proceed, for example, with the running kehre, the (one legged take-off) fencer kehre or the (one legged take-off) fencer tucked wende, just like with the tucked wende, as described before.

183

Neck Kip, Head Kip
and Piked Front Handspring (Yamashita) ***

For children that are weak in, or afraid of, vaulting, neck kips, head kips, as well as piked front handsprings over a side box or side horse, they can be supported during take-off between spring board and box by reaching around the thighs, which allows them to lift the center of gravity (seat) over the head. In the (neck, head, hand) support phase, two different spotter grips, the turn grip forward and the turn-carry-grip, can be applied.

a) The turn grip forward

The turn grip forward can be placed on the upper arm for smaller children. Therefore the children grab tightly with both hands from the beginning, and keep this grip until the end of the movement. The movement may not be supported and steered ideally, but with this grip at the upper arms, the upper body can be erected and therefore kept in a leaning forward position during the landing into the vertical (Fig. 158.1-158.3).

Fig. 158.1-158.3: Roll upon the box and neck kip

Because the term "turn grip forward" is too abstract for children, in order to associate it with a grip technique, a pictorial suggestion that has worked quite well is: the "crocodile grip" (compare here the explanations for "front flip" with the mini-tramp, p. 192 f.).

Optical control for the correctness of the grip onset

The thumbs of the spotter hands point forward downward when reaching around in turn grip (Fig. 171.4, p. 193). The spotter function becomes obvious when the spotters turn their hands back to themselves with this grip onset, holding on to the upper arm: The gymnast lowers the upper body forward downward and "bows".

Important hints

The spotting children must:

* stand very close, almost underneath the gymnast

* turn the gymnast at head height

* keep the arms during landing at their head height (and not what is usually done, pressing the arms down, because the spotters are thinking about the landing).

Fig. 159.1-159.3: Roll forward through a kip position

Working on the grip in overseeable, slowed down and safe situations

The children should test and firm up this grip

* at first at the standing partner (Fig. 171.1-171.4) with game like test exercises

* then at a box at hip height, from a rolling onto the box, through a brief kip position (Fig. 159.1-159.3)

* then by rolling onto the box from a run (Fig. 160), for weak vaulters two spotters stand by the spring board, reach around the thighs, lifting and pushing the seat overhead

Fig. 160: Rolling onto a box

185

- then by rolling into kip position on a long box, to flipping off the box, and stretching to a stand

- then at last the neck kip over the side box (Fig. 158.1-158.3)

Variation:
Head kip and piked front handspring.

b)   Further developed turn-grip: Turn-carry-grip
The older spotters form a lane in front of the gymnast.

- The close hand points with the palm of the hand upward (hand gesture: "Please, it's your turn!") and moves toward the gymnast. Then, they go between upper arm and neck to the shoulder in order to lift the gymnast off the floor, and thereafter erect the upper body. With the landing the hand may slide further forward in order to hook on the shoulder ("throw out the anchor"). This prevents the body from falling forward.

- The far hand goes under the center of gravity (seat) and lifts the body's center during the beginning of the movement, in order to then lower it again when erecting the upper body. This simultaneously offers a resistive force for a supported point while erecting the upper body for the landing (Fig. 161).

Because front handsprings off the various vaults are usually performed by falling forward, the "seat" hand changes to the upper arm and reaches around it from the front. With this "clamping" of both hands, the upper body can be kept ideally upright. Because these spotter actions are complex they can only be executed by advanced spotters or teacher/coaches.

Fig. 161: Head kip as a front handspring

Hint:

A support of the lumbar region with the far hand has to be corrected, because:

- it increases the possibility of hyperlordosis

- the frequent force impact of the spotters hands into the arched back is not healthy

- the support point thus lies above the center of gravity, and carrying can't be done ideally, nor can the other hand create a resistive force for the erection of the upper body

Front Handspring ****

- Two spotters stand between spring board and vault at the height of the board (not at the vault). The hand that is close to the vaulter goes, with the palm pointing upward (hand gesture: "Please, it's your turn!"), toward the vaulter. With the jump onto the board this hand goes under the thigh in order to support the rotational upward phase of the legs (as accelerating force aiming past the center of gravity). The far hand goes to the stomach in order to steer the body to the vault (Fig. 162). With these two separated "pressure points" of the supporting hands, an extension of the hips is made easier.

Fig. 162

Fig. 163

- Two more spotters stand behind the vault. The hand close to the apparatus turns, with the palm of the hand upward (hand gesture: "Please, it's your turn!"), in order to approach the shoulder girdle of the gymnast. This hand goes to the shoulder between upper arm and neck in order to assist the support, while the far hand carries the gymnast under the center of gravity (seat) (Fig. 163) (tip: this can easily be practiced with

1   2   3   4

Fig. 164.1-164.4: Front handspring: spotting in a team

the kick to handstand). With the pushing up and raising of the upper body through the first spotter hand, the spotter hands lower to the seat (Fig. 164.4). The "shoulder hands" go further forward, hook in ("throw out the anchor") for the landing, or the "seat hands" quickly change to the front toward the upper arms (Fig. 165). With this "clamping" of the upper arms, the shoulder girdle (and therefore the head) can be kept upright. This is an ideal aid in order to prevent a bending forward (or closing forward). Reaching around the hips affects the body by folding together through the arm resistance of the spotters, and is therefore not advised.

Reduction of spotting

- Depending on the ability level, first reduce by one spotter between spring board and vault, later on the second spotter.

- The spotters mostly support the above only with described grip "as much as necessary, as little as possible", especially for landings.

- Finally, standing three feet from the vault, they only support the stand-up phase with one hand on the back, and with the hand close to the body at the stomach, to prevent a forward fall.

- Once the vault is mastered, one to two spotters secure only with widely spread arms.

Fig. 165: Landing

189

3   Mini-Tramp

Straight Jumps *

Two children stand on each side of the mini-tramp, on two small boxes (panel mats), and reach one hand each to the gymnast as a balancing aid (Fig. 166).

Fig. 166: Straight jumps

Jumps Onto and Over a Box (panel mats) **

Two spotters stand opposite each other on the box and offer the far hand to the gymnast for support, the close hand helps by lifting under the armpit (Fig. 167), and depending on the situation, pulling the gymnast up and over (for example over two side boxes).

Fig. 167: Over a box

Securing the Landing *

For the straight jump, tuck jump and pike jump, the spotters stand on a cushioning mat, the close foot placed onto the frame of the mini-tramp. With the close hand they catch the gymnast at the back, away from the trampoline, and prevent a fall backward on the tramp during landing. The far hand secures at the stomach to prevent a fall forward (Fig. 168).

For increasing safety of the jumpers, the spotters stand approximately three feet away from the tramp, and only secure the landing at stomach and back ("sandwich").

Fig. 168: "Sandwich"

Exception: Securing landings for straddle jumps

In order to avoid injuries because of the sideward, upward legs, spread in a straddle (or pike) jump, the spotters stand to the side of the mini-tramp and merely secure at the back, preventing a fall backward onto the apparatus during landing (Fig. 169). Another spotter (a third) can additionally secure a possible forward fall at the end of the mat. He will try to secure the stomach of the gymnast – standing to the side.

Fig. 169: Straddle jumps

Mini-tramp as take-off aid for support jumps **

If the mini-tramp is being used as a take-off aid for supported jumps over boxes, panel mats or the vault, then the same spotter grips come into play as described for the vaulting apparatus.

Salto Forward/Somersault (Front Flip) ****

At this point an important warning has to be made about letting children perform a salto forward without a careful methodical approach. Most often the result of allowing such attempts prematurely would be a "forward-roll-without-hands", too close to the frame of the trampoline. Children like to mention very often that they have already done this with a previous teacher, or that they can do this already. Under no circumstances must the teacher be guided by this, or rely on the accuracy of these statements.

Introductory exercise: Turn-over Forward Tucked and Turn Grip Forward **/***

Regarding the terminology: Turning over forward

The pre-step for the front flip is the turning over forward tucked (also without tramp). The "turn over forward" for transversal rotations always includes that the body is kept "in the air" through the hang (for example on high bar or rings) or support (see above), as well as through partner support on the upper arm (see photo 18 and 36). In contrast to this, the salto movement is an unsupported rotation of the body in the air. For the turning over forward one applies the turn grip forward.

Description of the spotter grip: Turn grip forward

Standing on the bed of the tramp, two spotters stand with one foot on the frame, sideways in front of the gymnast. For the grip onset the performing child must keep the arms lowered, diagonally backward. The spotters go with the hand close to the gymnast, with the palm of the hand

Fig. 170.1-170.3: Turn-over and turn grip

turned out from the front under the upper arm (Fig. 170.1). This allows the gymnast to be lifted off the floor (or tramp) during the start of the movement, and to initiate rotation by pressing the upper arms from behind above, and then forward. The far hand of the gymnast is turned inward and reaches from the top around to the back side of the upper arm (Fig. 170.2). In the course of the rotary movement the second helper hand carries the gymnast, and secures him from falling backward at the landing (Fig. 170.3).

Introduction of the grip onset for children: the "Crocodile grip"

Fig. 171.1-171.4: "Crocodile grip"

From the beginning the children reach around the upper arms. Because the term "turn grip forward" is too abstract to associate it with a grip technique, a pictorial suggestion has proved to work very well. The following verbal aid is suggested for children's gymnastics:

The spotting children are opposite each other – sideways in front of the gymnast. They clap their hands and thus form a

"hand lane" in which the thumbs point upward (Fig. 171.1). Thereafter, both thumbs will, at first, be turned toward the gymnast (Fig. 171.2), then further in the direction of the floor (Fig. 171.3). The fingers of the "hand lane" open for the clamping of the upper arm, like the "crocodile that snaps" (Fig. 171.4).

Verbal accompaniment: "(1) Clap (2) Turn– thumbs to the gymnast (3) Jaws open (4) Jaws snap closed." Therefore, the children like to refer to the spotter grip as "crocodile grip", and is, as such, easily remembered.

Working on the grip in overseeable, slowed down and safe situations
The children should:
* solidify the grip in game type test exercises with a motionless partner (Fig. 171.1-171.4)
* then apply it during a forward roll on the high box

The turn grip forward enables the spotting children to support the course of the movement from beginning to end, and to control the dynamic movement of the "salto" (here it's still turning over forward) in an accompanying manner (compare also the movement description for front handsprings over vaults, p. 187).

This is only partly going to be the case with the following salto spotting grips. Therefore the following spotter grips should only be executed by experienced spotters or by the teacher/coach. The second condition for the salto movement, with regard to the following salto spotter grips, requires sufficient motor and mental preparation of the gymnast through the turn over forward in its raw form.

Hints for working with the mini-tramp
For mini-tramp the onset of the turn grip is at first trained through straight jumps with arms held back. This should be repeated before each of the following, more difficult tasks, which means, when the turn over forward with turn-grip aid is being performed:
* out of numerous bounces on the tramp
* from a jump off a box into the tramp
* from a run

Spotter grip for salto forward/front somersault (front flip) ****

Two spotters stand in front of the practicing child, extend the close arm toward him, palm of the hand turned toward the body under the stomach. Thus, the gymnast can be lifted, and rotation can be initiated. The second, far hand, waits for the rotation to begin, and supports this forward rotation as the longer lever arm from the rotation point (center of gravity) through pressure on the back. With crossed spotter arms, now anatomically considered a clamp, the landing child is secured to a stand after the salto forward (flip) (Fig. 172).

Variation for securing the landing:

Shortly before the landing, experienced spotters can secure the landing, ("sandwich") through changing of the hands, with the hand close to the apparatus behind the back, and the far hand in front of the stomach. This is later

Fig. 172: Salto forward (front flip)

on the "correct" way of securing the landing, without prior interference into the course of the movement, as is described in the following.

Hint:

It's advisable to use two eight inch mats when practicing the forward salto. Thus, the landing height is not only slightly above the height of the mini-tramp frame, but the spotters are elevated and can more easily reach in and correct.

Safety spot for the salto forward/front somersault (front flip) ****

Two spotting children are standing opposite each other, approximately two feet away from the tramp on a mat elevation. They wait for the salto rotation to begin and go with the opening for the landing, with the close hand on the back in order to protect the child from falling backward onto the tramp. The far hand is placed in front of the stomach in order to prevent a falling forward (Fig. 173, p. 196).

Hint:

In case there is only one mat in length instead of two, there should be two more "emergency" spotters at the end of the mat, in order to secure a possible "forward shooting" after the salto, that couldn't be caught or sufficiently secured by the first two spotters. In order to prevent a fall off the mat, they act as a stopping aid with the far hand reaching for the stomach.

Fig. 173: Salto forward: safety spot

Salto Backward (Back Flip) ****

All methodical implications with regard to approaching the skill, as well as spotter grips, generally equal those for the salto forward (front flip).

Introductory exercise:
Turn-over Backward Tucked with Spotter Grip:
Turn Grip Backward **/****

Description of the spotter grip: Turn grip backward

For the turn over backward one applies the turn grip backward (for the introduction of the turn grip see above under "neck kip" (p. 184) and "front flip" (p. 192), for which the approach to the turn grip forward is transferable to the turn grip backward).

Fig. 174.1-174.2

Two spotters stand sideways next to the gymnast who keeps his arms parallel in front, hands at shoulder height. When performed on a mini-tramp the spotters put one foot on the frame and stand behind the gymnast.

The spotters go with the hand close to the gymnast under the upper arm; the palm of the hand is turned outward (Fig. 174.1). Thus, the gymnast can be lifted from the floor (tramp) once he

initiates the movement. Rotation can be initiated by forcing the upper arms upward, backward (Fig. 174.2). The hand that is farthest from the gymnast is held, with the palm of the hand turned inward downward, and reaches from above around the upper arm, the thumb almost grasping into the armpit (Fig. 174.1). In the course of the rotational movement this second hand carries the practicing child in the downward phase of the movement, and secures him from falling back on the landing by tightly grabbing with the other hand.

Introduction of the grip onset with children

From the beginning the children should reach with both hands around the upper arms. The following verbal aid – as for the turn grip forward (see above) – has proved to be helpful: The spotting children stand opposite each other, sideways behind the gymnast.

They clap their hands and form an "hand lane", with the thumbs pointing upward. Thereupon, both thumbs should, at first, be turned toward the gymnast, then further in the direction of the floor. The fingers of the hand lane open in order to reach around the upper arm (like "the crocodile that snaps", see Fig. 171, p. 193, but transferred onto backward movements).

Verbal accompaniment for children: (see p. 194)

Visual control for the correctness of the grip onset

The thumbs of the spotters point downward during the clamping and in turn grip backward. When the spotters turn their hands back again, with this onset of the grip while holding on to the upper arm, the spotter function becomes obvious; the gymnast must lift the arms upward, backward.

Working on the grip in overseeable, slowed down and safe situations

The children should try this grip:
*   with a standing partner
*   then, with someone performing a backward roll on a high box with landing behind the box
*   finally, by running up the wall, followed by a turn over backward tucked in the air. As a playful variation one can try the "throw flip" backward (from a solid, small elevation, done onto a cushioning mat). A third spotter offers, with folded hands under a lifted foot, an elevated push-off plane for the throw flip

Important hints:
The spotting children must:

- stand very close, almost under the gymnast

- turn the gymnast at head height

- hold the arms with the landing at head height (and not, what is usually done, pushing the arms, and therefore the upper body downward, because the spotters are only thinking about the landing)

Hints for working on mini-tramp
On mini-tramp the turn grip onset is at first practiced through straight jumps, with arms held in front. This should be repeated for the next, more difficult task, when the turn over backward is performed from numerous preceding bounces on the tramp, or from a jump off a high box onto the tramp.

The turn grip backward enables the children to support the movement of the gymnast from beginning to end, to accompany and support until the safe finish of the landing, and to control the dynamic movement of the "salto" (at this point it's still turning over backward).

This is only going to be the case for the following salto spotter grips. Therefore, the following spotter grips should only be executed by teachers/coaches or experienced, older spotters. A second condition for the following salto spotter grips is that the gymnast should be able to perform the salto movement (turn over backward) in its raw form, through sufficient preparatory exercises.

Spotter grips for salto backward (back flip) *
Two spotting children stand in front of the gymnast, extend the close arm toward the practicing child and with the palm of the hand turned toward the body, under the seat, close to the thigh (Fig. 175.1). Thus, the gymnast can be lifted and rotation initiated. It's favorable to reach with the far hand from above onto the waist of the shorts in order to carry or pull the gymnast away from the apparatus. Once the gymnast is overhead he can be carried on top of the fist (Fig. 175.2-175.3). Later on, when the back flip can be performed from a push off the box, the second, far hand will only support through pressure under the seat, close to the back, while waiting for the onset of the rotation (Fig. 176).

Variation for the grip onset of the far hand:

- The far hand reaches into a "salto belt"/ inner tube from a bicycle, or something similar that's strapped around the hips. Without changing the grip the gymnast is held until the landing.

Fig. 175.1-175-3

- Taken from competitive trampoline we apply the spotting with the far hand at the shoulder (from behind, between neck and upper arm), in order to create a higher, almost fixed point of rotation after the take-off. This should only be executed with older and more experienced spotters.

Variation for securing the landing:

Experienced spotters can secure the landing by changing their hands, with the close hand at the front, and the far hand at the back ("sandwich"), shortly before the landing. This is, later on, also the "correct" way of securing the landing without any prior interference with the movement, as is described in the following.

Safety spot for salto backward (back flip) ****

If the gymnast can perform the back flip safely with a spot at the seat, only the landing remains to be secured. Two spotting children stand opposite each other, with a

Fig. 176

two foot distance from the trampoline. They wait for the salto movement to start, and go with the opening of the landing with the close hand to the stomach in order to prevent a fall toward the trampoline. The far hand goes on the back in order to prevent the gymnast from falling backward.

Back Handspring (Back Flip/Flic-Flac)

Spotters kneel down or stand tightly behind the gymnast. Both hands toward the center of gravity (=seat).

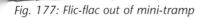

Fig. 177: Flic-flac out of mini-tramp

4 Hang and Support Apparatus (Including Climbing Poles and Ropes)
(Low and High Bar, Uneven Bars, Parallel Bars, Rings, Trapeze, Ropes)

Hanging and Swinging *

Two children reach around the wrist of a hanging person (Fig. 178a).

Variation at the low bar in reaching height:
The far hand grasps around the wrist, the near hand helps to amplify the swing at the shoulder (Fig. 178b).

Fig. 178a/b: Hanging and swinging

Chin-up on Hang Apparatus *

When chin-ups are done as a fitness exercise, one to two children reach around the thighs of the gymnast. Almost effortlessly the gymnast can experience and repeat numerous chin-ups (in various grips and with different leg positions) (Fig. 179).

Fig. 179: Chin-up

Climbing Up the Rope **

A gymnast jumps into bent arm hang and grabs the rope with the inner foot and instep with tucked legs (climbing lock). A spotter grabs the rope with both hands underneath the feet. The gymnast reaches further up and can now push upward, off the hands of the spotter, which serve as resistance (Fig. 180). Arms can pull gently into bent hang.

Fig. 180: Climbing

Front Support *

There is no support necessary for the front support on a bar or on parallel bars, even though the use of the support grip can be observed over and over again. The front support is an exercise for learning to develop support strength. In case of failure, or giving up early, there are no concerns with regard to the safety of the child. On parallel bars though, we need to make sure that the bars are lower than the shoulder height of the standing gymnast (if necessary raise the standing surface for the gymnast). In order to experience a "tall" front support, two spotting children can reach around the thighs and push the supporting child up.

Jump to Front Support *

Two children stand at take-off height and reach around the thighs of the gymnast. The gymnast bounces twice on the spot and then jumps up to support. The spotting children lift the center of gravity of the gymnast with support grip at the thigh.

Swinging in Front Support on Parallel Bars *

The children can't effectively support each other on parallel bars because the actions of the spotting hands are different. Additionally, the fast succession of technical execution cannot be followed adequately. Thus the spotter activities are too complex to be transferred efficiently to the ability level of the children.

When swinging in support is being practiced, the teacher or coach can help to steer the movement by using one hand at the upper arm as a supportive, resistant force for the shifting of the shoulder girdle. The other hand supports the up-swinging center of gravity. If, for example, the emphasis is on the front swing, the hand goes behind the upper arm at arm height. The spotter reaches around it (fingers in the armpit) and prevents the shoulder girdle from leaning back too far, and therefore collapsing backward during the forward swing, through the resistance offered. The hand on the side of the forward swinging body supports the up-swinging movement under the seat (Fig. 181).

If the emphasis is on the back swing, the hands reach exactly reversed and support accordingly in the reverse (Fig. 182).

Kehre on Parallel Bars **

An older spotter stands at support height on the landing side of the bars and reaches from the front, with the the hand nearer the front, (creating a resistive force for the other hand) onto the close upper arm. He shifts the shoulder girdle for the forward, over-the-bar-swing in a supportive manner and pulls the gymnast away from the bar lane. The rear closer hand goes under the center of gravity to the seat. It lifts and steers the body away from and over the bar lane (Fig. 181).

Fig. 181: Kehre

Wende on Parallel Bars **

Similar to the Kehre, the gymnast is being led out of the bar lane, except that he is supported at the stomach instead of the back (Fig. 182).

Fig. 182: Wende

Circular Tuck Wende on Parallel Bars ****

The teacher stands at support height on the landing side (also support side). As with the kehre, one hand goes from the front onto the upper arm in order to support and initiate the shifting of the support arm shoulder out of the bar lane. Simultaneously this spotter hand creates a resistive force by reaching around the upper arm for the turn-push-movement of the second hand against the side of the seat (center of gravity) of the tucked gymnast. If this hand goes further under the thigh the tight tucked position can be supported (Fig. 183a). If this hand goes into the hip bend the center of gravity can be lifted and steered more easily (Fig. 183b). Thus, the gymnast is turned around the support arm over both bars, in tucked position.

Fig. 183a/b: Circular tuck wende

Slide Down Forward from Front Support into Hang (-stand) *

Two spotters carry the gymnast downward at the seat, standing close under the center of gravity.

Turn-over Backward *

a

b

Weaker students stretch one foot to a spotter. The spotter lifts this foot to the bar so that the gymnast can push off the bar for further rotation (Fig. 184a). Some children let their foot (and thus, the center of gravity) be lifted, only so that they can swing with the second foot under the bar in order to continue going backward (Fig. 184b). In case holding strength is lacking, the wrists can additionally be secured (Fig. 178, p. 201).

Fig. 184a/b: Turn over backwards

Turn-over Backward on High Hang Apparatus (High Bar, Rings, Trapeze) **

On high rings, on the trapeze and on the high bars, two spotters or the teacher assist with the turn over to inverted tuck hang by standing in front of the gymnast, "hooking" the close hands behind the upper arms/shoulder (Fig. 185, 186.1) (fixation) and pushing the seat (center of gravity) with the far hand

Fig. 185: Grip for Turn-over

1   2

Fig. 186.1-186.2: Fixation and pushing

over the head (Fig. 186.2). When the gymnast continues to turn for the landing, the "seat hand" goes immediately to the upper arm in order to secure the landing with support grip.

Turn-over Forward *

In general there is no spotting necessary. Exceptions have to be made when the gymnast has no sense for the movement, or the basic strength prerequisites are not there. The teacher may then assist with a push under the thighs/seat.

Turn-over Forward from an Elevation into a (Brief) Piked, Inverted Kip Hang on Rings **

The gymnast is in tuck stand on the elevation (high box), the arms are led backward over the side (like a breast stroke in swimming) and hang from in the shoulders. Two spotting children stand opposite each other under the practicing child. The hand farthest from the box initiates the rolling movement at the head, the close hand pushes under the calves of the tucked legs, into the rolling movement to inverted hang (kip hang).

Pullover **

Two spotters stand at a right angle in front of the bar and reach with both hands for the seat (Fig. 187). With the take-off for the pullover they go close to the gymnast and carry the stomach of the gymnast to the bar, with both hands at the seat (Fig. 188.2, see photo p. 200).

Fig. 187: Spotting with both hands

Fig. 188.1-188.2: Pullover with two spotters

Hint:

For the pullover on the higher bar, the spotters stand slightly elevated on boxes in order to push the gymnast's center of gravity sufficiently upwards (Fig. 189).

Fig. 189: Standing elevated

Pullover on the Trapeze *

If the pullover is performed on a "moving" apparatus, it's not just the seat alone that needs to be supported, because the body tends to move away with the apparatus when lifted and pushed under the center of gravity. Two spotting children can stand by the trapeze, holding on to it with the close hand (c. h.) as a resistive force, while the far hand (f. h.) helps to lift up the center of gravity under the seat onto the trapeze (Fig. 190).

Fig. 190: On the trapeze

Long Hang Pullover on High Bar and High Trapeze ***

a) "Baby giant"

(In the upward phase, shoulder girdle remains, with decreasing arm-trunk-angle, almost under the hanging point.)

Two spotting children stand at the return point. The gymnast swings forward in long hang. As was described for the turn over on rings (see Fig. 187, 188, p. 205), the helping close hands go from the side between the neck and upper arm into the shoulder, and prevent the swinging back by "hooking in" and holding back (the spotter hand creates a resistive force). The far hand goes underneath the seat and lifts the center of gravity with a "slap" (accelerated spotter hand) overhead, onto the bar/trapeze.

With this kind of spotting the hooking in of the backside of the knees (knee hang) and the fly-away out of a forward swing can be supported. The latter though should be spotted by the teacher or coach.

b) Long hang pullover on high bar in preparation for the giant swing

(In the upward movement of the body the shoulder girdle is taken upward, along with the opening of the arm-trunk-angle.)

Four spotters stand on high boxes that are arranged as a box lane, exactly under the high bar.

Two spotters guide the cast from a support position into long hang, with the far hand under the thigh (the "V" created by the thumb and pointer finger goes under the thigh, the inside of the hand lies at the thigh) and the close hand under the stomach (Fig. 191.1).

Fig. 191.1

Fig. 191.2

The two other spotters in front of the bar have already reached around the wrist from underneath the bar, to secure the grip and to provide rotational aid (Fig. 191.1). In the upward phase they reach around the shoulder in order to lift the body into the vertical (Fig. 191.2). If the body tends to fall back in the upward phase, the far hand goes to the back in order to give resistance (Fig. 192).

Fig. 192

When swinging over the bar, the first two spotters catch the gymnast by grabbing under his thighs, and carry him with the near hand on the stomach to support or hang (Fig. 191.2).

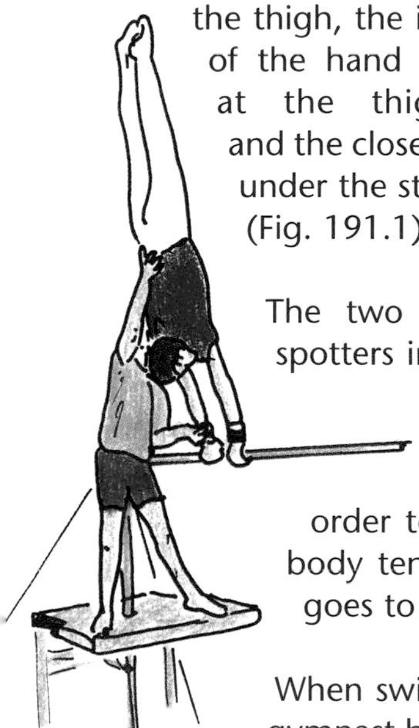

Clear Hip Circle to Support, Hang and Handstand on a Bar at Head Height

Two spotters stand in front of the bar, waiting for the initiation of the hip circle movement. They grab on as early as possible, with both hands at the shoulders (hands form a "bowl"), and pull and push the gymnast into the

vertical over the bar, supporting the extension of the arms. If in the upward phase of the movement the body tends to fall back, the far hand is placed on the back, providing resistance.

If the clear hip circle finishes in support or hang, two more spotters catch the gymnast's thighs with the far hand when the body moves over the bar, and carry and guide him into long hang or to support, with the additional support of the near hand under the stomach.

If the clear hip circle is performed to handstand, the two other spotters need to stand elevated on high boxes, with one leg standing over the bar. They reach as early as possible around the legs (ideally the thighs) in order to guide and lift into the handstand.

Back Hip Circle **

The gymnast is in front support, two spotters stand in front of the bar facing each other. Both hands go toward the seat in order to keep the center of gravity at the bar during the hip circle movement. The far hand can be placed on the thigh in order to amplify the rotation (Fig. 193.1-193.2).

Fig. 193.1-193.2: Back hip circle

Front Hip Circle ***

The gymnast is in support. Two spotting children stand opposite each other in front of the bar, and go with the back of the hand onto the back of the gymnast in order to support the downward forward rotation. After passing the horizontal, the second hand goes to the center of gravity (seat), the first hand now also slides closer to the center of gravity. In the upward phase both hands now push the center of gravity at the seat against the bar. In order to do this they need to go a little bit under the bar.

Swinging in Knee Hang on a Bar *

Two spotters reach around each wrist of the swinging gymnast.

Seat Up-swing from a Knee Hang *

Two spotters reach around the upper arms, pushing the hanging gymnast twice to get the swing started, and assist energetically the third swing, turning the gymnast backward upward to a sitting position on the bar.

Seat Circle **

Two spotters stand in front of the bar, grab the wrist with the near hand under the bar so that they can see the back of their own hand; thumb clamps the wrist (securing the wrist and for rotational aid, Fig. 194). As early as possible, the far hand goes, after the initial rotation, onto the upper arm/shoulder (Fig. 195.1), and erects the upper body. For this the spotters must be close in front and under the gymnast (Fig. 195.2).

Fig. 194: Securing the wrist

Fig. 195.1-195.2: Seat circle: spotters erect the body

Fig. 196: Securing the wrist

Front Stride Circle/"Mill Circle" ***

Two spotters stand behind the bar and grasp the wrist of the gymnast with the close hand underneath the bar (Fig. 196, 197.1). The far hand helps to erect the shoulder during the upward movement (Fig. 197.2), until arrival in a sitting position on the bar with legs spread (Fig. 197.3). Attention: make sure the gymnast is in reverse grip.

1   2   3

Fig. 197.1-197.3: Front stride circle

Knee Up-swing **

One spotter is in front of the bar, on the side of the swinging leg. The gymnast hangs only from one knee. The far hand of the spotter pushes during the upward movement down onto the swing leg of the gymnast. The second hand pushes the center of gravity, at the seat, against the bar. A second spotter, behind the bar, can help the gymnast up, with both hands at the seat (Fig. 198).

Fig. 198: Knee up-swing

Knee Hang *

Assistance for getting into a knee hang, with one or two legs, is the same as for turning over backward (Fig. 184a/b p. 204). The securing in knee hang happens through light, downward pressure against the lower legs (Fig. 95, p. 133).

Swinging in Knee Hang **

Two spotters stand in front of the bar and secure the squeezing of the bar through the knee bend, by pushing the gymnast's lower legs down on the instep with both hands (Fig. 199) – later on only with the far hand (f. h.) (Fig. 200.1).

Fig. 199

Knee Hang Swing Dismount "Napoleon" **

Two spotters stand in front of the bar and secure the squeezing of the bar through the knee bend with the far hand, while pushing down the lower legs on the instep. The hand close (c. h.) to the gymnast goes under the bar, onto the stomach of the hanging child, and thus lifts the body early and energetically into horizontal (Fig. 200.2).

With the opening of the knee bend, for the lowering of the feet, the "foot-instep hand" (f. h.) quickly goes to the back, in order to prevent a fall back to the bar. The spotters now stand with crossed arms and hold the gymnast like a clamp for the landing (Fig. 200.3).

Fig. 200.1-200.3: Knee hang swing dismount

Spotter grips for the slowed down carrying out of the knee hang into horizontal for jumping down: Two spotters reach with the close arm underneath the stomach of the hanging child, the far hand goes into the armpit. The gymnast gets carried forward, upward into horizontal, so that tension in the knee joints is created (prevents slipping off early). With the lowering of the feet the hand goes from the stomach to behind the upper arm thus preventing a fall backward.

Knee Hang Swing Dismount off the Low Bar on the Uneven Bars, with Grip on the High Bar ***

Two spotters in front of the low bar firmly fix the knee bend with the far hand, and put the near hand on the stomach for the latter swing amplification. Two more spotters stand inside the bar lane and reach around the upper arms of the gymnast. The gymnast now releases his grip and the spotters carry him into the horizontal (hips extend). After a small lift the spotters release the upper arms and the gymnast starts to swing down, while being secured by the front spotters, until he reaches a standing position (Fig. 201.1-201.3).

Fig. 201.1-201.3: Knee hang swing dismount

Hint:

As additional help, an aid for orientation, and for purposes of intensifying the practice process, through the inclusion of possibly many children, another spotter can stand in front of the landing area and offer his hands to hold on to. This spot can be used later on for landing security.

Safety spot for skilled knee hang swing dismounts: One to two children secure the landing at stomach and back.

Knee Hang Swing Dismount off the Trapeze **

The spotting here is similar to the spot given on the bar. At the trapeze the children can secure the movement by grasping the hands if enough movement safety is given – just like when they practice in the play ground. They stand in front/under the swinging gymnast, pull him by the hands until the return point of the swing, and thus keep holding the body up when the gymnast jumps down (Fig. 202).

Fig. 202: Safety grip

Under-Swing from Standing Position *, on the Uneven Bars over the Low Bar and from Front Support **

Landing security can be given by one or two children at the front and back (Fig. 203.1).

Fig. 203.1: Landing security *Fig. 203.2-203.3: Preventing a fall forward*

Older students or the teacher/coach can guide the movement by reaching for the gymnast's shoulder with the close hand (Fig. 203.2), while he is still standing, in order to erect the upper body in the final phase of the movement; the far hand goes to the seat and carries the body in the main part of the movement forward, upward. The "seat hand" then changes during the landing, from the front onto the upper arm, in order to prevent a fall forward. (Fig. 203.3). If the under-swing is performed on the uneven bars over the low bar, the spotters need to stand elevated (on a box) and support and steer similarly to the last described spotting procedure, at the shoulder and under the center of gravity. Two more spotters can secure the landing at the front and back ("sandwich").

For the under-swing from support, the same spotting technique on the shoulder and the seat applies as well. From the beginning the far hand pushes the body upward (standing very close) and the near hand waits until it can get to the shoulder. With the lowering of the center of gravity, and the resistive force of the far "seat hand" under the center of gravity, the close "shoulder hand" erects the upper body. The landing is secured, for example, as in front handsprings (Fig. 8.4, 8.5, p. 33).

Sole Circle Dismount ***

If the piked sole circle dismount is developed on a low bar, the inner hand reaches for the wrist from the front underneath the bar, the far hand supports in the upward phase under the seat. The wrist is held until the landing in order to keep the upper body erect. For the first step, a third spotter can reach from behind around the hips, and lifts the gymnast backward upward for swing amplification and for the extension of the arm-trunk-angle (preferably gymnast and spotters should stand on an elevation).

Change of spotting technique:

If the gymnast has a strong grip, the near hand can reach from outside onto the shoulder (almost between upper arm and neck), in order to carry the upper body upward and erect it, while the far hand is still carrying under the center of gravity (seat). This way of spotting is also used when the sole circle under-swing is done with a grip change from low bar to high bar to long hang.

For the landing after the sole circle dismount from a low bar, the "seat hand" goes from the front to the upper arm in order to clamp with the other arm, preventing a fall forward (Fig. 203.3).

If the sole circle dismount is performed from a high bar one or two spotters can slow down the downward movement or catch the seat and legs (for the piked variation, legs closed).

Securing the landing:

When the gymnast is able to perform the sole circle dismount skillfully, one or two spotters catch only the back and front for the landing.

Leg Lift over the Bar to a Sit *

After swinging one leg over from support, a spotter in front of the bar grasps the foot and keeps the leg of the gymnast in place. The second leg can now lift over to a sitting position without any problems (Fig. 204).

Fig. 204: Swinging legs from support to sitting position

One or Two Legged Stem Rise on Uneven Bars **

The gymnast is in "tuck-hang-stand" on the low bar with grip on the high bar. Two spotters stand – if necessary on boxes – and reach with both hands under the center of gravity. The hand close to the low bar supports under the thighs, creating a resistive force for the gymnast in the final phase of the movement. With the stem rise movement to support, the spotters guide the center of gravity (hips), the shortest way possible to the bar. For the one legged stem rise, in which one leg is held in kip position by the high bar, the spotter holds on this side under the thigh, the other leg remains vertical to the bar from the beginning of the movement (Fig. 205).

Fig. 205: Stem rise

Stem Rise from a Long Hang Sit on the Low Bar with Grip on the High Bar ***

Two spotters stand at leg height, grasping the feet with the far hand from the top, the near hand goes under the center of gravity. After two preliminarly swings the gymnast is lifted to support by carrying the center of gravity upward and pressing the legs down (long lever), while executing a stem movement with the arms.

Lowering Backward into Inverted Kip Hang and Reverse Kip to a Sit on Uneven Bars ***

Two spotters stand behind the bar or the gymnast and carry him, with the close hand at the seat and the far hand at the shoulder (Fig. 206.1), downward into a piked, inverted hang (kip hang) (Fig. 206.2).

Fig. 206.1-206.2: Lowering backward

Kip Up to Straddle Sit, Upper Arm Kip and Upper Arm Roll on Parallel Bars ***

Two spotters stand behind the bar or the gymnast and carry him, with the near hand at the shoulder and the far hand at the seat, up to hand support height. For the upper arm roll the same positioning of the hands applies for holding the body at bar height. With the beginning of the up-swing/kip, the hand underneath the seat guides the center of gravity to the bar, and the hand on the shoulder pushes with this long lever arm the upper body energetically into the vertical (Fig. 207).

Fig. 207: Kip-up

Elgrip Kip ***

The gymnast stands with elgrip (reverse grip), rearward to the bar. Two spotters stand on the other side of the bar, reaching with their close hands from outside to the shoulder in order to support the introductory forward rotation into inverted hang. The far hand goes against the vertical thigh in order to steer the legs into the horizontal from an inverted hang. After the inverted hang is reached, the hands change for spotting, with the near hand

under the center of gravity (seat) and the far hand under the shoulder girdle. With the up-swing into the inverted hang, the hand under the seat leads the center of gravity to the bar, and the shoulder hand pushes the upper body energetically into vertical with this long lever arm (Fig. 207, p. 217).

Kehre with 1/4 Turn from Inverted Hang ***

After lowering into the inverted hang (see above), the gymnast performs a quarter turn during the upward phase of the movement through the release of one hand. One spotter stands at the rear, reaches with the hands in the up-swing phase under the armpits, then lifts and turns the gymnast into the quarter turn.

Kip-up from Inverted Hang or Drop Kip from Front Support Back to Front Support ****

The spotters stand in front of the bar and keep the close hand under the center of gravity, and the far hand against the thigh. They carry and guide the gymnast into the kip hang and support him again, as in the final phase of the kip ("kip push"), to kip and stem up to support (Fig. 208).

Fig. 208: Start to kip-up

Suspension and Long Hang Kip on Uneven Bars ****

The gymnast sits on the low bar and reaches back, grabbing the high bar. Two spotters stand on an elevation and reach with both hands under the center of gravity. The hand close to the low bar supports and carries under the thigh, creating a resistive force for the gymnast to push against in the final phase. With the stemming (kipping) up to front support, the spotters guide the center of gravity in the shortest way to the bar (Fig. 208).

Hint:

The spotters do not place the far hand (which is underneath the high bar) on the shoulder, because in this decisive phase, due to the height, it's no longer possible to give upward support.

Glide and Long Hang Kip on High Bar, Uneven Bars and Parallel Bars ****

The spotters stand in front of the bar or under the parallel bars. With the start of the glide the far hand goes underneath the legs (depending on the strength, more under the calves or thighs). In the stem phase the hand underneath the thighs serves as a resistive force for the support of the legs. From the beginning, the close hand goes under the center of gravity (seat) and lifts it toward the axis of rotation (the bar) (Fig. 208).

Hint: At the beginning of the learning process for the glide kip, a third spotter, who is standing behind the gymnast, can lift the center of gravity at the hips, upward backward and, therefore, also extend the arm-trunk angle. Preferably both the gymnast and the third spotter should stand elevated.

Upper Arm Stand on Parallel Bars and Forward Roll **

Two spotters stand elevated, right and left, on support, or later at shoulder height of the gymnast. With the lifting, or up-swing phase of the legs, the hand close to the feet goes under the thigh in order to lift. The second hand reaches around the thigh from behind and prevents the gymnast from falling over. With the established support grip ("clamp grip") the gymnast is held vertical (Fig. 209.1). If this is followed by a forward roll the spotters slow down the carrying into the movement by pulling on the thighs (Fig. 209.2).

Fig. 209.1

Fig. 209.2

Back Swing to Handstand on Parallel Bars ****

The spotters stand elevated, just as for the upper arm stand (on boxes or panel mats) and lift during the up-swing phase under the thigh, and finally in support grip (clamp grip) at the thigh (Fig. 210).

When more movement safety is needed by the gymnast, a teacher can reach around the upper arm from the front on the support arm side, in order to prevent too much forward shifting of the shoulder girdle (resistive force for second spotter hand). The other hand lifts the center of gravity at the bottom side of the body or at the stomach, the hips or the thighs (depending on the height of the parallel-bars and size of the gymnast). For the finish of the movement the spotting hand can go to the support arm, but only from behind, in order to secure balance while in handstand.

Fig. 210: Handstand

Dislocate from an Inverted Pike Hang/ Kip Hang to Long Hang on Swinging Rings ****

Two adult spotters stand at the return point of the back swing of the rings and receive the legs supportingly with the far hand on the front side of the thighs, and pull and carry the body in a guiding manner into horizontal. With the opening of the hip angle at the front side of the body, the second hand interacts supportingly a little later (Fig. 211.1). This means, the "stomach hand" goes along the legs into the arm lane under the stomach, waiting for the initiation of the extension. With the carrying of the body under the stomach and under the thighs, the body is carried under the fixation point, and the shoulder girdle now has less weight burden for the bringing forward of the arms (Fig. 211.2).

This should be practiced methodically on rings at head height, long enough for the movement safety to be established, because the spotters should be at

the body right at the beginning of the movement. Spotting from boxes is no longer a necessity when changing to rings that are high enough to hang.

A large number of teachers prefer the support at the shoulders, because of the early contact with the body at the beginning of the movement. Due to the spotter's wide arm positioning at the shoulders and legs, the body cannot be carried ideally in order to relieve the weight of the hang. This type of spotting only works on high rings, because on head-high rings one cannot carry under the shoulder girdle, nor can the rings be moved away from the spotters.

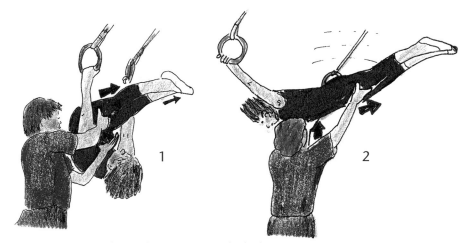

Fig. 211.1-211.2: Dislocate from an inverted pike hang

5 BALANCE APPARATUS
(Benches, Rounded Beam, Balance Beam, Bars at very low height, Ropes and more)

Gymnastics Elements on the Beam *

For gymnastics elements on narrow support surfaces, as for example for walking, bouncing, hopping, split and cat leaps, for pivot turns, as well as for static elements, such as scales or V-seat, one to two spotters offer balancing aid through hand grasping. While, at first, two spotters may be assisting, in the further course of practice only one spotter reaches his hand to the gymnast. Spotting turns into movement accompaniment when the gymnast merely touches the hand of the spotter, just being connected by the fingers (see photo on the opposite page). Then, only the "pointer finger" is offered. Finally, only one child secures with a widely held arm (see Fig. 117-119, p. 161).

Forward Roll ***

Two spotters stand in front of the gymnast and go with the near hand to the upper arm. The "V" between thumb and pointer finger is placed at the upper arm, the inside of the hand points upward (the hand performs a movement, as if saying "Please, it's your turn!"). During the movement the far hand slides over the seat onto the back of the thigh. The gymnast remains in kip position and is held by the spotters as described (Fig. 212.1-212.3). Thereafter the gymnast is assisted in reaching a standing position.

Fig. 212.1-212.3: Forward roll with two spotters

The rolling movement has to be self-initiated (the forward roll on a line or widened beam/bench is a learning prerequisite). For nervous children the teacher or coach can help to lift the seat from behind and guide it over the head.

Reduction of spotting:

A spotter stands in front of the gymnast and waits with extended arms for the rolling gymnast (for the nervous children the spotter needs to stand very close). With rolling into kip position the spotter reaches around the hips/seat and guides the center of gravity over the beam and corrects deviations (Fig. 213).

Fig. 213: Forward roll with one spotter

Prerequisite:

The gymnast must perform the forward roll slowly (head placed between feet and hands).

For faster rolling movements, the spotters now only assist from the side in order to offer his hands to hold on to (Fig. 214).

Free Forward Roll ****

The gymnast is in squat stand, with arms held to the side. Two spotters stand sideways by the beam (facing the beam) and go with the hand close to

Fig. 214: Guiding into stand

the beam under the shoulder, and reach the far hand to the hand of the rolling gymnast. With this grip that stabilizes the shoulder girdle, the gymnast rolls forward and is assisted into stand.

Scissor Handstand and Handstand ***

Two spotters stand at the height of the hand support location (if beam is high, on a box) and lift the center of gravity (stomach) with the near hand at the hips into vertical. With the far hand at the seat/lumbar area, they

prevent a falling over. By reaching around the hips, the scissor handstand can then be kept in balance, without obstructing the scissoring of the legs. When the swing leg lowers for landing, the spotters keep the center of gravity over the support location (over the hands), long enough for the first foot to reach the apparatus (Fig. 215). Hereafter the spotters secure through hand grasping, until the gymnast reaches a safe stand.

Fig. 215: Handstand

With kicking up to a handstand and the closure of the legs into a holding position, (which is different from a scissor handstand), one can also reach for the thighs for spotting (same for floor).

Spotting reduction on high beam:

The spotters stand at the height of the hand support location and place the hand that is furthest from the gymnast from the front onto the upper arm, and prevent a pushing forward of the shoulders (this is also a resistive force for the second hand). The close hand goes underneath the stomach or to the hips, and lifts the center of gravity over the hands, keeping it there until the landing leg touches the beam, and finally helps with balancing until the body is erect.

Cartwheel ****

Two older spotters stand shoulder to shoulder (on boxes, if the beam is high) at the height of the hand placement. Both spotters reach from the back around the hips (spotter arms cross over here) of the gymnast (fingers of the gymnast must point in the direction of the spotters). The spotter close to the gymnast is mainly responsible for the up-swing phase (close hand to the gymnast lifts the hips), the second spotter primarily secures the landing (far hand in the hip bend keeps the seat over the beam) (see Fig. 133, p. 171).

Spotting reduction:

Only one spotter lifts, steers and holds the hips over the beam.

Mounts from a Side Stand

Front Support and Lifting of One Leg Over, with a Turn to Cross Sit *

No spotting is necessary here.

Tuck Wende onto the Beam **

For children that do not succeed with a squat on, in the form of a tuck wende, the teacher can stand at the take-off location and exert a turn-push-aid. The hand close to the beam supports the upper arm, the other hand supports the upward-turn-movement at the seat (see spotting at the box, Fig. 157, p. 183; see photo, p. 180).

If the gymnast can get onto the beam on his own, one spotter prevents a falling over on the opposite side of the beam from the take-off, by giving resistance with one hand at the shoulder and the other hand at the seat (center of gravity).

Mounts from a Cross Stand

Squat On, Straddle On, Squat Through to Sit, One Legged Squat Through to Sit **

For all supported mounts from side stand, the spotter grip that needs to be applied is the same. As for support jumps, two spotters stand shoulder to shoulder and reach around the upper arm with support grip. The spotters prevent the gymnast from falling backward with this spotter grip, by pulling the shoulder girdle over the beam. Furthermore, they counteract a falling over in case the gymnast uses an intensive swing.

Fig. 216

Additional help can be given to those children that do not succeed with the squat on through two spotters that are positioned at the take-off location. With the gymnast's take-off they reach with both hands around the thighs, thus lifting the center of gravity (seat), and support the arrival into the squat position (Fig. 216, 217).

Squat On from Cross Stand at the End of the Beam ***

Two spotters stand by the beam and assist with support grip. Two more spotters reach around the thighs during take-off (this is at first done from standing, with a little bounce), lift the seat and lead the gymnast simultaneously into the squat position, with strongly bent hips (Fig. 216).

With an increase in movement safety, only two spotters support with the far hand from the front at the upper arm. The

Fig. 217

near hand goes under the seat/thigh. With this spotter grip the gymnast is pulled into the squat onto the beam (Fig. 217).

Squat On from Cross Stand without Support of the Hands ****

Two spotters stand next to the gymnast, support their inner hand from behind under the armpit/upper arm of the gymnast and extend the outer hand under the gymnast's hand, so that the gymnast can find support on it. Gymnast and spotters run together toward the beam, and with take-off, the spotters carry him up to a stand on the beam (Fig. 218).

Fig. 218

Fig. 219

Run On from Cross Stand ****

Spotting is the same as described above for the squat on without support (Fig. 219).

Mounts from Diagonal Stand

Run On with Support of One Hand from Diagonal Stand **

One spotter stands on the outside of the gymnast who is positioned diagonally in front of the beam, reaching with the close hand under the armpit, the far hand reaches under the free hand of the gymnast. The spotter now runs with the gymnast to the beam and carries him with the take-off onto the beam, securing the landing on the beam with the same spotter grip (balancing aid, Fig. 220).

Fig. 220

Unsupported Run On from Diagonal Stand ***

With an increase in movement safety the run-on from a diagonal stand can also be done with a similar spotting technique, but without support of the hand.

Dismounts

Jump Downs *

One to two spotters can, if necessary, secure the landing with one hand on the front and one on the back (see Fig. 120, 121, p. 162).

Round-off **

• Movement steering from low apparatus

One to two spotters reach around the hips and lead the round-off through a brief side handstand. At this point they prevent a falling over and push against the hips for the remaining 1/4 turn so that the gymnast can land (see round-off as basic exercise for floor, see Fig. 134, p. 172).

• Movement assistance from high apparatus

One spotter stands on the side of the stem leg (this is, where the first hand is going to be placed). With the near hand to the gymnast, he goes into the "arm lane" of the supporting gymnast. The spotter reaches from inside to the closely placed second arm, shifts the shoulder girdle supportingly in the direction of the movement, over the point of support, away from the beam.

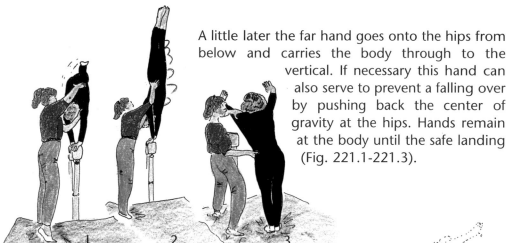

A little later the far hand goes onto the hips from below and carries the body through to the vertical. If necessary this hand can also serve to prevent a falling over by pushing back the center of gravity at the hips. Hands remain at the body until the safe landing (Fig. 221.1-221.3).

Fig. 221.1-221.3: Round-off from the beam

- ### Securing the landing after the round-off

With an increase in movement safety, only one spotter needs to stand on the stem leg side and secures front and back during the landing (Fig. 222).

Fig. 222: Securing the landing

Front Handspring ***

The spotters stand shoulder to shoulder facing the end of the beam. For the handspring movements the hand close to the beam goes between the neck and upper arm into the shoulder (the hand makes a gesture, as if saying "Please, it's your turn!"). The second hand goes under the center of gravity and carries under the seat. This supported spot turns into a resistive force for the erection of the upper body (simultaneously lowering the center of gravity) (see Fig. 8.1-8.5, p. 33).

Securing the landing

- With the landing each hand on the shoulder now moves further forward, in order to hook in ("throw out the anchor") and to prevent a falling forward.
- An even safer method is the grasping of the upper arm with the far hand, the one that previously supported the seat which goes with the landing, from the front onto the upper arm (see Fig. 8, p. 33 and Fig. 164, p. 189).

- Once the front handspring is mastered, a "sandwich" spot on front and back is sufficient to secure the landing. For this the spotter stands about two feet away from the end of the beam.

Hint:

Nervous gymnasts can be supported additionally by two spotters right and left (standing on a box), who facilitate the kick-up into the handstand at the swing leg or at the torso (hip bend). Often the mere presence of a spotter serves as psychological aid.

Salto Forward (Front Flip) ****

See description and explanation on floor and mini-tramp (see Fig. 146, p. 178 and Fig. 172, p. 195). The teacher/coach is the only spotter.

Salto Backward (Back Flip) ****

See description and explanation for mini-tramp (see Fig. 175, 176, p. 199). The teacher or coach is the only spotter.

Side Aerial to Landing with Legs Together ****

The teacher or coach stands on the stem leg side at the end of the high beam and reaches with the "V" (thumb and pointer finger) of the opened hand into the hip bend of the stem leg. With the initiation of the side aerial (non-supported round-off), the second hand goes to the opposite hip side and guides the center of gravity through to vertical. The gymnast is now firmly grasped by the hips and can be assisted with landing.

Securing of the landing after the side aerial:

With an increase in movement safety only one spotter on the stem leg side is necessary to secure front and back.

Front Aerial Off Beam ****

The gymnast lowers into lunge position with arms spread to the side. Two spotters reach with their hands to the upper arms and support them as the axis of rotation at knee height of the gymnast (not higher!). The gymnast flips over and the spotters keep holding onto the arms until landing.

Securing the landing after the front aerial:

With an increase in movement safety, one to two spotters only secure at front and back during landing.

APPENDIX

A   Spotting and Securing for School Gymnastics

Because the guidelines from North-Rhine-Westfalia are widely detailed in numerous volumes, they are shown as exemplary curricular suggestions.

1   Spotting and Securing within the Framework of Pedagogical Reasoning

The guidelines for physical education in the schools of North-Rhine-Westfalia formulate nine basic tasks. The fifth one contains the aspect of self-sufficiency, in and for the sport, with the students self-organization of sports situations. The students shall be enabled to:

• co- or self-create the surrounding conditions

• give mutual assistance, advice and correction

• act autonomously and self-responsibly

With this assignment it's every physical education teacher's duty, equal to bringing about skills, to guide toward spotting and securing amongst the students. Through spotting and securing the class works in small groups. This brings about innumerable situations of supporting each other, advising, correcting, as well as solving problems. This form of continuous, creative communication provides a substantial contribution for the development of autonomy, self-acting and self-responsibility.

The Bavarian constitution in Germany says that schools have the duty, "not only to create knowledge and ability, but also heart and character." Spotting means cooperation in helping and accepting help.

2   Care and Supervision Duties of the Teacher

The care and supervision duty demands the teacher to prevent accidents, with simultaneous orientation for pedagogical assignments. Educating the students to act independently, must not jeopardize the safety in school sport.

Care and supervision duty demands from the teacher, amongst other things, "to awaken the consciousness for safety of the students through thoughtful instruction and familiarization with an orderly, circumspect and self-responsible conduct (as well as) . . . to meet special safety precautions in individual cases."

This does not demand from the teacher to execute each assistance and safety spot himself. To the contrary, the inclusion of the students for spotting is emphasized through the guidelines. This happens, based on professional instruction from the teacher, and thus requires subject specific knowledge. "In certain cases, for example with nervous students, or for exercises with particularly hazardous moments, it is usually crucial that the teacher him-/herself supervises the course of the exercise, and takes over the necessary spotting or securing of the movement."

3   Spotting and Securing in Gymnastics

The guidelines and curriculum for physical education in the schools in North-Rhine-Westfalia bring into sharper focus the significance of the inclusion of spotting in the gymnastics lesson for this sports field.

> "For movement-intensified gymnastics lessons and for assuring
> quick learning, at the same time excluding risks of accidents,
> as well as furthering of the autonomy of the student,
> qualified spotting of the students is a necessary prerequisite."

"During the course of the teaching units a justified movement and situation assistance shall be developed out of simple spotter actions, so that more difficult and riskier forms of movement are learned only with appropriate social maturity and technical spotter ability of the students . . ."

4 Spotting and Securing at Elementary Level

In one guideline for schools in Germany specific suggestions are given with regard to the elementary level for each class level, which include the acquisition of knowledge.

The first two school years in gymnastics contain "playful confrontation with each apparatus and their peculiarities, along with the discovery of action possibilities." This happens primarily through gymnastics-specific basic movement forms (climbing, balancing, jumping...) that do not require partner assistance for the achievement of the posed tasks. At this level preparatory exercises for later spotter actions are introduced.

The curriculum of another part of Germany foresees tasks for this class level that contain experience with partners and the group:

• Movement tasks shall be solved with a partner, or in the group.

• As a preparation for later spotting, the students learn hand reaching and readiness for balancing, climbing over and jumping down from apparatus.

• Common set-up and take down of the equipment (mats, balance beams, boxes) furthers the consciousness of cooperation and mutual assistance.

At the third class level the students learn specific basic skills that require spotter actions. On floor, the kicking up to handstand, the pullover on a low bar and the straddle jump over the box are worked on in groups of three (see an overview on the next page from a German guideline, p. 234).

Development of spotting assistance at the elementary level

Spotter actions/grips (including the acquisition of knowledge)
1 Spotter conduct: Creation of prerequisites (p. 72-137) **Spotter grips:** • Balancing aid (Fig. 117-119, p. 161) • Grip securing on high bar: Swinging in tuck hang (Fig. 178, p. 201) • Securing of knee hang: Pushing down of lower leg (Fig. 199, p. 211)
2 Spotter action: Choice of location: Gymnast must not be obstructed through spotting **Spotter grips:** • Grip securing on high bar: Tucked turn over backward (Fig. 184, p. 204) • Push aid for pull-over (with both hands at the seat) (Fig. 188, p. 205) • Support grip for kneeling onto a box (Fig. 150, 151, p. 181) • Securing landing for under-swing at front and back (Fig. 203, p. 213)
3 General: • Significance of spotting and securing shall be highlighted with regard to succeeding in gymnastics. • Spotting assistance shall be worked on in small groups. **Spotter conduct:** • Creating awareness of the moving toward each other, grasping, walking and moving along during spotting (e.g. p. 144) • Walk along aid (for example when balancing) • Self-acting spotter change • Spotter location can only be vacated when new spotter is ready **Spotter grips:** • Support grip at the thigh: both hands reach around the thigh for a handstand (Fig. 101, 102, p. 142f.) • Push-turn aid for a knee up-swing (Fig. 198, p. 210) • Support grip at the upper arm for a squat on onto a box, and a straddle over (Fig. 150, 151, p. 181) • Securing landing for under swing at front and back (Fig. 203, p. 213)
4 General: Spotter activities from the third class level are repeated and solidified. **Spotter conduct:** • Recognizing spotting reduction for safety spotting • Group work shall lead to, at times, teacher independent gymnastics activities **Spotter grips:** • Support grip for a handstand forward roll (Fig. 130, p. 170) • Push-turn aid with both hands at the seat for a pull-over on uneven-bars (Fig. 189, p. 206) • Carry grip on shoulders and seat for the under-swing over the low bar on uneven-bars (Fig. 203, p. 213) • Support grip on the upper arm for the one legged squat on onto a beam • Support grip for squat on and squat through and for the straddle jump on vault (Fig. 154, p. 182)

B   Manual Guidance in Peak Performance Gymnastics

by Alexandra Pizzera

Psychological Institute
of the German Sport University Cologne

One of the main goals in peak performance gymnastics is the acquisition of new complex motor skills. The main process underlying this acquisition of new movements in all fields of motor behavior is called motor learning. The high requirements especially in the competition orientated field of gymnastics make it necessary to optimize this learning process. Gymnasts have to face several different problems during their career. They have to learn risky new skills in a very short time period and *perform* these new skills with a high movement quality in a transfer situation such as a competition, *without* the help of supporting hands by the coach. Furthermore, gymnasts are usually very young or in the age of puberty. They have to deal with their anxiety, with pressure and excessive demands. To support these difficult learning processes coaches often use *manual guidance*, in this book referred to as spotting and securing. Although manual guidance is naturally used during the training process in gymnastics, it is up to today still based on experience and therefore conducted in an intuitive manner. But what exactly are the effects of manual guidance *in peak performance* gymnastics? Which components are influenced in particular? Is manual guidance really effective? What roles do emotions of a gymnast play during the learning process? To try to solve the discrepancies between theory and applied theory, research needs to be taken into account, conducting different studies to examine the applied, widespread use of manual guidance in an experimental setting, based on fundamental theories.

In the field of gymnastics only two studies were conducted. Mc Auley (1985) *found a significant influence of manual guidance on performance in a transfer situation, on anxiety and self-efficacy*. He used the front roll as a mount onto the beam as the task to be learned. Velentzas, Niessen & Heinen, (2006)

came to similar results. In their study, where gymnasts had to learn a front flip as a dismount off the balance beam, the effectiveness of manual guidance was allocated.

As can be seen, researchers come to different results, which can be due to different tasks and different methodologies being used in the experimental designs. But when taking a look at peak performance athletes, who have to show their performance at a high level of expertise without the help of manual guidance, it becomes obvious that researchers should not only take the influence of manual guidance on current movement quality into account, but also on movement quality in a transfer situation (competition without manual guidance). Furthermore, emotions of athletes and their link to manual guidance, especially in risky sports as gymnastics, should be addressed.

Consequently, in my work the goal was to examine the influence of manual guidance on different phases of the learning process, but also on anxiety and self-efficacy. Furthermore, the underlying mechanisms of the influence of manual guidance on emotions are to be found out.

A study with 14 gymnasts (9-19 years old) was conducted with a time period of 5 weeks. The task was to learn a gainer salto from the side of the beam as a dismount (see below).

At the beginning a gymnastic specific motor test was conducted to detect the individual motor performance. Then, each week a methodical step was introduced, being conducted twice per week. Overall there were 4 methodical steps whereas in the fifth week, the gymnasts were asked to perform the criteria movement themselves. During the learning process a protocol was taken, detecting the intensity (without, less or much) and amount of manual guidance being used and external feedback being given.

Manual guidance was provided by placing the hands under the center of gravity in order to support rotation and height and to slightly push the gymnast away from the beam (see left).

In addition, a questionnaire was distributed to all gymnasts after each methodical step to detect the self-perceived anxiety and self-efficacy. Furthermore, the gymnasts were filmed after each methodical step for performance rating of external judging experts.

Special attention was paid to the *emotions* of the gymnasts, addressing the question whether they were *positively influenced by manual guidance* and therefore, *movement quality* would increase. Furthermore, the amount and intensity of manual guidance was seen as an important aspect, connecting to the three differentiated forms (spotting, manual movement accompaniment and securing), introduced by Ilona E. Gerling.

This work is therefore seen as a support to optimize the learning process in the applied field of sports. The goal is to provide athletes, coaches and advisers with practical tips, based on scientific insights.

The results of the study show that 6 of the 14 gymnasts were able to perform the gainer salto by themselves whereas 8 gymnasts still needed manual guidance. The gymnasts who showed a good basic movement quality had the tendency to ask less for manual guidance and also showed higher movement quality when performing the gainer salto. At this point I would like to emphasize **the importance of basic training for gymnasts**. Another important aspect deriving from the experiment is the *amount and intensity* of manual guidance. As proposed by Ilona E. Gerling that movement accompaniment should follow the motto "as much as necessary – as little as possible", **the experiment showed that manual guidance can be effective in the acquisition phase**, but **should gradually be removed as performance increases, if in the transfer situation the movement is to be performed without support**. To realize this, **the coach should have a high ability of securing and a lot of spotting experience.** He/she then is able to fulfill the requirements of "sensitive neuromuscular adaptation" (p. 30) to the degree of skill ability of the gymnast.

When taking a look at the emotions, it can be seen that the **somatic anxiety** (body reaction due to fear) of the gymnasts significantly **decreased with manual guidance**. This could lead to **better performance** and **higher self-efficacy**, because it was shown that **movement quality increased when performed with manual guidance**.

The explanations for the findings just mentioned are numerous and interesting for the applied field.

- First of all, manual guidance is able to provide the gymnast with the **correct movement pattern** when having to learn a **difficult technique**.

- Furthermore, **it can decrease movement error**, leading to **fewer injuries**. But also fewer errors can creep in, which usually are very hard to overcome, once they have become a habit.

- Due to the decrease of **anxiety** through manual guidance, **the gymnast has more resources for focused attention** (Velentzas, Niessen & Heinen, 2006). He/She does not have to worry about injuring him-/herself and therefore is able to focus more on the essential parts of the movement.

Due to the differentiation of manual guidance, the criticism of researchers that problem-solving cannot be learned when using manual guidance, is herewith declined. Gymnasts are able to make movement experience and perception, as long as the coach is able to show **a feeling of sensitivity while providing manual guidance**. When facing the age and puberty problem of young gymnast, manual guidance can help provide them with a sense of achievement so that their self-efficacy increases and therefore, fun and joy for gymnastics remains high.

Literature

Armstrong, T. R. (1970). *Training for the production of memorized movement patterns* (Tech. Rep. No. 26). Ann Arbor, Michigan: University of Michigan, Department of Psychology.

Martens, R., Vealey, R. S. & Burton, D. (1990). Competitive Anxiety in Sport. Champaign: Human Kinetics.

Mc Auley, E. (1985). Modeling and Self-efficacy: A Test of Bandura's Model. *Journal of Sport Psychology, 7*, 283-295.

Schmidt, R. A. & Lee, T. D. (2005). *Motor Control and Learning* (4th Ed.). Champaign: Human Kinetics.

Schmidt, R. A. & Wrisberg, C. A. (2000). *Motor Learning and Performance* (2nd Ed.). Champaign: Human Kinetics.

Singer, R. N., Pease, D. (1974). A Comparison of Discovery Learning and Guided Instructional Strategies on motor skill Learning, Retention, and Transfer. *Research Quarterly, 47*, 788-796.

Velentzas, K., Niessen, A., Heinen, T. (2006). *Optimierung von Bewegungen durch individualisierte manuelle Bewegungsführung*. In F. Ehrlenspiel, J. Beckmann, S. Maier, C. Heiss & D. Waldenmayer (Hrsg.), Diagnostik und Intervention – Bridging the gap (S. 141). Czwalina Verlag Hamburg.

Wulf, G.; Toole, T. (1999). Physical Assistance Devices in Complex Motor Skill Learning: Benefits of a Self-Controlled Practice Schedule. *Research Quarterly for Exercise and Sport (70)* 3, 265-272.

Picture Legend to Page 17

Figure I: Securing of the wrist for "mill sideways with one arm"

Figure II: Securing of the wrist for "down swing backward from a sit into hang, with back facing the apparatus"

Figure III: Securing of the wrist for the "beginning of the giant swing backward"

Figure IV: Support grip for the "up-swing backward"

Figure V: Securing of the knee bend and swing amplification at the stomach for the "knee hang from both knees"

Figure VI: Push-turn aid for a "single leg shoot through; one leg is between the arms"

Figure VII: Support grip at the upper arms ". . . for a straddle forward"

Figure VIII: Safety spot for a "scale at one knee, with stemming of the other foot against the bar"

Figure IX: Safety spot for the "rear end jump on a side box to cross sit"

Figure I-IX: "Assistance" from Eiselen, 1848

Literature References

1.   Cooperative and Competive Games (Chapter B I 1.1)

Döbler, H. & Döbler, E. (1978). *Kleine Spiele*. Berlin: VEB Volk und Wissen.
   Hagedorn, G. (1987). *Spielen*. rororo Sport Bd. 8603, Reinbek:
   Rowohlt Taschenbuch Verlag.

Huberich, P. & Huberich, U. (1988). *Spiele für die Gruppe*. Verlag Quelle &
   Meyer, Heidelberg/ Wiesbaden.

Mitterbauer, G. & Schmid, G. (1985). *300 Bewegungsspiele*. Innsbruck:
   Steiger Verlag.

Schmid, G. (1991). *Abenteuer Spielstunden*. Innsbruck: Steiger Verlag.

2.   Acrobatics and Circus Tricks (Chapter B I. 1.3)

Bardel, B. (1992). *„Akrobatik mit Kindern"*. In: Bardel, B.: Circus – Bewegungskünste mit Kindern. Moers: edition aragon, S. 14-23.

Blume, M (2007[8]). *Akrobatik mit Kindern und Jugendlichen in Schule und Verein*.
   Aachen: Meyer & Meyer Verlag.

Blume, M. (2008[4]). *Akrobatik*; Training - Technik - Inzenierung. Aachen:
   Meyer & Meyer Verlag.

Fodero, J. M. & Furblur, E. E. (1989). *Creating Gymnastic Pyramids and
   Balances*; A safe and fun approach! Leisure Press, Human Kinetics
   Publishers, Inc., Champaign, Illinios , USA (ISBN 0-88011-308-1).

Gaal, J. (1994). *Bewegungskünste – Zirkuskünste*. Jonglage, Einradfahren,
   Akrobatik für Schule, Verein und Freizeit, Schorndorf.

Grabowiecki, U. (1992). *„Akrobatik"*. In: Ballreich, R. & Grabowiecki U. von:
   Zirkus-Spielen. Ein Handbuch für Artistik, Akrobatik, Jonglieren,
   Äquilibristik, Improvisieren und Clownspielen. Stuttgart: Hirzel
   Verlag, S. 36-110.

Huismann, B. & Huismann, G. (1988). *Akrobatik – Vom Anfänger zum Könner*.
   Reinbek: Rowohlt-Verlag.

3.   Spotting, Guiding and Securing

Becker, W. & Bockhorst, R. & Haberstroh, Kl. (1995). *Hilfen zum Helfen*. Helfergriffe für das Turnen in der Schule. Gemeindeunfallversicherungsverband (GUVV) Westfalen Lippe, Münster.

Carr, G. A. (1980). *Safety in Gymnastics*. North Vancouver, B. C.: Hancock House Publishers Ltd. ISBN 978-0-888-39054-7

Garufi, G. (1994). Movement Assistance/Assistance and Spotting. In: Fédération Internationale de Gymnastique (FIG) (publisher): Manual Training of FIG-certificate Instructors in General Gymnastics. 88-91.

Gerling, I. E. (2006[3]). *Kinder turnen: Helfen und Sichern*. Aachen: Meyer & Meyer Sportverlag.

George, G. S. (1980): Biomechanics of Women's Gymnastics. Enlewood Cliffs, N.J. 07632: Prentice-Hall, Inc. Capt.: Spotting and Safety Procedures, p. 203-214.

Herrmann, K., (1981). *Methodik des Helfens und Sicherns im Gerätturnen*. Schriftenreihe zur Praxis der Leibeserziehung und des Sports, Bd. 122, Schorndorf: Hofmann Verlag.

Wettstone, E. (editor). (1979[2]). Gymnastics *Safety* Manual. The Official Manual of the United States Gymnastics *Safety* Association. The Pennsylvania State University Press. University Park and London, p. 26-31, 102.

4.   Extended List of Gymnastics Literature

Bucher, W. (Hrsg.). (1992). *1008 Spiel- und Übungsformen im Gerätturnen* (6. Aufl. mit Lehrbeilage „Schüler helfen Schüler"). Verlag Hofmann, Schorndorf.

Australian Gymnastics Federation INC (editor) (1991). *AUSSIE Gym Fun Lesson Plans Level 1 and 2* Australian Gymnastics Federation, Melbourne around (order: A. G.F - INC Melbourne., Suite 1/135 Sturt ST., Southbank Vic 3006, PH.: + 03-96820600, Fax + 03-96820677.

Collins, J. (Producer) (1991). *Gymnastics: What's in it. A practical guide for the beginner gymnastics coach.* (A Resource to supplement the

Australian Gymnastic Federation's Level 0 Coaching Course). Australian Gymnastics Federation INC (editor): Melbourne. ISBN 0-9592505-8-1.

Fédération Internationale de Gymnastique (FIG) (editor). (1998). Manual Training of FIG-certificate Intructors in General Gymnastics, Fédération Internationale de Gymnastique (FIG) (publisher) Order: FIG, Rue des Oeuches 10, Case Postale 359, CH 2740 Moutier, Schweiz (Fax +41.32.494.64.19).

Gerling, I. E. & Steuri, R. (1994). Fundamental Forms of Movement in Apparatus Gymnastics. In: Fédération Internationale de Gymnastique (FIG). (publisher). 23-51.

Gerling, I. E. (2005^2). *Gerätturnen für Fortgeschrittene. Band 1: Boden und Schwebebalken.* Aachen: Meyer & Meyer Sportverlag.

Gerling, I. E. (2008^2). *Gerätturnen für Fortgeschrittene. Band 2: Sprung-, Hang- und Stützgeräte.* Aachen: Meyer & Meyer Sportverlag.

Gerling, I. E. (2008^6). Basisbuch Gerätturnen. Aachen: Meyer & Meyer Sportverlag.

Lee, M. (editor). (1993). *Coaching Children in Sport* – Principles and Practice. E & FN Spon, Chapman & Hall, London, England ISBN 0-419-18250-0.

Schembri, G. (1991). *AUSSIE Gym Fun* – A Resource for Schools & Clubs, Australian Gymnastics Federation, Melbourne. ISBN 0-646-08750-9.

Schembri, G. (1983). *Introductory Gymnastics* – A Guide for Coaches and Teachers. Australian Gymnastics Federation, Melbourne ISBN 0-646-08750-9.

Still, Colin (1990). *BAGA Women's Gymnastics Manual.* West Yorkshire, England: Springfield Books Limited, ISBN 0-947655-28-X.

United States Gymnastics Federation (editor). (1992). American Coaching Effectiveness Program: *Rookie Coaches Gymnastics Guide,* Human Kinetics Publishers, Champaign, Illinois, USA; ISBN 0-87322-390-X.

Credits:

Cover Design: Sabine Groten, Germany

Cover Photos: Prof. Dr. Jens Kleinert;
                   ©Fotolia.com, mag;
                   ©Fotolia.com, Germany

Photography: Ilona E. Gerling, Germany

Illustrations: Ilona E. Gerling, Germany

GYMNASTICS
HOW TO CREATE CHAMPIONS

Learn from a world-class coach

Achieve remarkable results

ARKAEV · SUCHILIN

MEYER
& MEYER
SPORT

MEYER
& MEYER
SPORT

25 YEARS

Arkaev/Suchilin
**Gymnastics –
How to Create
Champions**

This book will be
invaluable to
coaches at all levels,
to university
departments of sports
theory and science
and to those
dedicated individuals
who really want to
increase their
knowledge of
gymnastics at the
highest level. The
author details how he
and his team
achieved these
remarkable results.

2nd edition
408 pages, full-color print
49 color and b/w photos,
72 illustrations, 22 tables
Paperback, 6^1/$_2$" x 9^1/$_4$"
ISBN: 978-1-84126-141-6
$ 29.00 US / $ 49.95 AUS
£ 22.95 UK/€ 27.95

The Sports Publisher

Carmen Himmerich
Keep Fit Exercises for Kids

Keep Fit Exercises includes fun exercises for children and adolescents age 6-14. This practiceoriented book enables professional and experienced work by trainers, sports instructors and physical education teachers alike. This book aims to offer assistance to all those people actively involved in putting a stop to postural deficiencies and defects among children and youths.

168 pages, full-color print
96 color photos, 5 illustrations
Paperback, 5³/₄" x 8¹/₄"
ISBN: 978-1-84126-150-8
$ 17.95 US / $ 29.95 AUS
£ 12.95 UK/€ 16.95

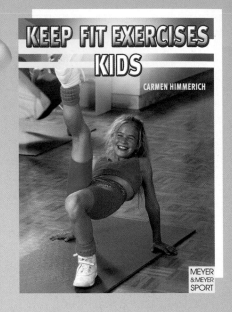

Jeff Galloway
Fit Kids
Smarter Kids

Olympian Jeff Galloway has seen the benefits of exercise on children, and has coached many to an active lifestyle. Fit kids perform better in school, have a better attitude, and tend to make better behavior choices. This is a guide for parents, teachers, youth leaders and anyone who wants to enhance the life of a child by introducing him or her to enjoyable exercise.

200 pages, full-color print
30 photos
Paperback, 6¹/₂" x 9¹/₄"
ISBN: 978-1-84126-193-5
$ 16.95 US / $ 29.95 AUS
£ 12.95 UK/€ 16.95

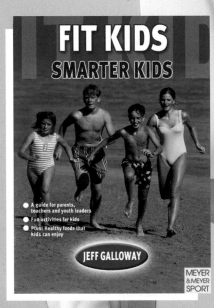

MEYER
& MEYER
SPORT

Let's move
Heidi Lindner (Ed.)
Great Games for Small Children

This starter book contains lots of tips on gymnastics work for parents working with children or for teachers working within schools and clubs. It contains all sorts of creative ideas using simple apparatus and will provide a comprehensive bank of general material to keep children amused and active.

96 pages, Two-color print
Numerous drawings
Paperback, 5³/₄" x 8¹/₄"
ISBN: 978-1-84126-064-8
$ 12.95 US / $ 19.95 AUS
£ 8.95 UK/€ 13.90

Let's move
Heidi Lindner (Ed.)
Animals, Animals, Animals

This is the first volume with a background theme to all the play and movement suggestions in its pages. Everything is based around the pretence of being or acting like the animals familiar to children within their learning environment. A Creative Corner is introduced, providing the children with mental stimulation within the animal theme.

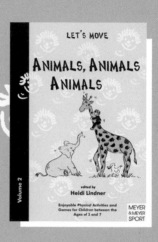

96 pages, Two-color print
Numerous drawings
Paperback, 5³/₄" x 8¹/₄"
ISBN: 978-1-84126-065-5
$ 12.95 US / $ 19.95 AUS
£ 8.95 UK/€ 13.90

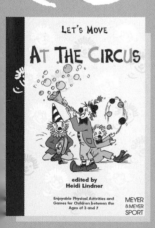

Let's move
Heidi Lindner (Ed.)
At the Circus

The topics for this volume are all from the wonderful world of the circus, which – with its clowns, acrobats and tightrope walkers – also fits perfectly into any carnival time. There is, for example, the *Story to Move to* "A Day at the Circus", and in the *Fun Activity* "In the Arena" we describe the best way to put on your own circus performance. Ideal for all exercise leaders and educators who play and do simple gymnastics with groups of children.

96 pages, Two-color print
Numerous drawings
Paperback, 5³/₄" x 8¹/₄"
ISBN: 978-1-84126-122-5
$ 12.95 US / $ 19.95 AUS
£ 8.95 UK/€ 13.90

Let's move
Heidi Lindner (Ed.)
On the Way

The mobility of participants in gymnastics with children and parents can be increased through the use of supports such as skateboards, balls and sticks! This book gives, among many other things, useful hints on how children and parents can get used to the skateboards and how using them can be practiced with the movement ideas presented in this volume, for the benefit of the children.

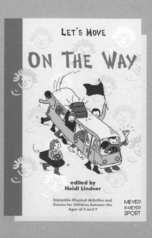

96 pages
Two-color print
Numerous drawings
Paperback, 5³/₄" x 8¹/₄"
ISBN: 978-1-84126-123-2
$ 12.95 US / $ 19.95 AUS
£ 8.95 UK/€ 13.90

MEYER & MEYER Sport | www.m-m-sports.com | sales@m-m-sports.com